ground beef,
chicken & turkey
...made simple

This edition published in 2012
LOVE FOOD is an imprint of Parragon Books Ltd

Parragon
Queen Street House
4 Queen Street
Bath BA1 1HE, UK

www.parragon.com/lovefood

ISBN: 978-1-4454-9959-8

Printed in China

Produced by Ivy Contract
Cover and new photography by Clive Bozzard-Hill
Cover and new home economy and food styling by Mitzie Wilson

Notes for the Reader

This book uses standard kitchen measuring spoons and cups. All spoon and cup measurements are level unless otherwise indicated. Unless otherwise stated, milk is assumed to be whole, butter is assumed to be salted, eggs are large, individual vegetables are medium, and pepper is freshly ground black pepper. Unless otherwise stated, all root vegetables should be washed and peeled before using.

For the best results, use a meat thermometer when cooking meat and poultry—check the latest USDA government guidelines for current advice.

Garnishes and serving suggestions are all optional and not necessarily included in the recipe ingredients or method. The times given are only an approximate guide. Preparation times differ according to the techniques used by different people and the cooking times may also vary from those given. Optional ingredients, variations, or serving suggestions have not been included in the calculations.

Recipes using raw or very lightly cooked eggs should be avoided by infants, the elderly, pregnant women, and people with weakened immune systems. Pregnant and breast-feeding women are advised to avoid eating peanuts and peanut products. People with nut allergies should be aware that some of the prepared ingredients used in the recipes in this book may contain nuts. Always check the packaging before use.

Picture Acknowledgments
The publisher would like to thank the following for permission to reproduce copyright material on the front cover:
Mediterranean chicken burger patty with lettuce © Gallo Images-Images of Africa/Getty images

ground beef,
chicken & turkey

introduction

Ground meat is one of the most widely used ingredients in modern cooking. It's the easiest, quickest meat you can cook with, and a great and economical way to feed family and friends. It's a simple, wholesome, and nutritious staple that freezes well and can be on the table in minutes when required. Ground meat tastes wonderful, and is actually something that nearly everyone likes.

Ground meat is versatile, and all kinds of meat can be ground, so it never gets boring. As well as being a source of protein, meat is an important source of iron, zinc, and vitamin B_{12}. Leaner ground beef is more expensive, but it contains less saturated fat and less weight is lost in cooking (from fat and water). If you use ground beef with a lot of fat, dry-fry it in a nonstick pan and then drain off the excess.

This book celebrates ground meat in all its forms. These 100 easy recipes include all our comfort food favorites, such as chili con carne, meatballs, and moussaka. There are also recipes with a spicy spin, from Moroccan ground meat to curry and burritos, plus a whole range of burgers and kabobs, from the classic to

the gourmet. Many dishes can be made ahead and reheated when you need them, making them the ideal solution for family midweek dinners or when entertaining.

Ground meat has always been popular, but most people have a somewhat limited repertoire of recipes. There's so much more to ground meat than a hamburger, and this book contains a range of delicious and inventive dishes that you may never have expected could be made from ground meat, such as dim sum, chicken, prosciutto and sun-dried tomato mini meatballs, Spanish rice, and turkey and chorizo empanadas. It is divided into chapters for rice and pasta dishes, burgers and kabobs, casseroles, spicy dishes, and small bites and nibbles. Within them you will find a wide selection of traditional and international recipes for all tastes and suitable for all occasions. From light lunch dishes to more impressive meals, this book will inspire you to try something a little different, and provide you with the confidence to create a ground meat dish that is something really special.

rice & pasta dishes

spanish rice

ingredients

serves 4

1½ tablespoons olive oil
1 onion, finely chopped
2 garlic cloves, finely chopped
1 red bell pepper, seeded and
  finely chopped
4 ounces chorizo sausage, chopped
8 ounces ground turkey
1⅓ cups long-grain rice
1 (14½-ounce) can diced tomatoes
pinch of saffron, steeped in a little
  lukewarm water
3 cups chicken stock
1 cup frozen peas
salt and pepper

method

1 Heat the oil in a large, shallow saucepan. Add the onion, garlic, red bell pepper, and chorizo and cook for 3–4 minutes.

2 Add the ground turkey and continue to cook for 2–3 minutes, using a wooden spoon to break up the meat. Stir in the rice, tomatoes, steeped saffron water, and stock and season with salt and pepper.

3 Cover and cook for 15–18 minutes, until the rice is tender. Stir in the peas and cook for 1–2 minutes, until heated through. Serve immediately.

moroccan rice

ingredients

serves 4

1 pound ground sirloin beef
1 onion, finely chopped
1 garlic clove, finely chopped
1 teaspoon cumin seeds
1 teaspoon ground cinnamon
2 teaspoons ground turmeric
3/4 cup coarsely chopped
    dried apricots
1/3 cup raisins
1 1/4 cups long-grain rice
2 1/2 cups beef stock
salt and pepper
2 tablespoons finely chopped
    fresh flat-leaf parsley and
    2 tablespoons toasted
    pine nuts, to garnish

method

1 Dry-fry the beef in a nonstick skillet for 4–5 minutes, until starting to brown. Add the onion and garlic and cook for an additional 1–2 minutes.

2 Add the cumin seeds, cinnamon, and turmeric and cook for 1–2 minutes, stirring continuously.

3 Add the apricots, raisins, rice, and stock and season with salt and pepper. Cover and cook for 15–18 minutes, until the rice is tender.

4 Sprinkle with the parsley and pine nuts and serve the dish immediately.

beef pilaf

ingredients

serves 4–6

½ cup olive oil
3 onions, finely chopped
3 garlic cloves, finely chopped
4⅓ cups long-grain rice
1 teaspoon ground cumin
1 teaspoon ground turmeric
1 teaspoon ground coriander
7¼ cups beef stock
1¼ pounds ground chuck beef
pinch of ground mace
1 teaspoon cumin seeds
2 tablespoons chopped fresh mint
1 stick butter
salt and pepper
fresh cilantro sprigs, to garnish

method

1 Heat 3 tablespoons of the oil in a saucepan. Add two-thirds of the onions and two-thirds of the garlic and cook over low heat, stirring occasionally, for 5 minutes, until softened. Add the rice, ground cumin, turmeric, and coriander and cook, stirring continuously, for 1 minute. Pour in the stock and bring to a boil. Stir well, reduce the heat, cover, and simmer for 15–20 minutes, until the rice is tender and the liquid has been absorbed.

2 Meanwhile, put the remaining onion, remaining garlic, the beef, mace, cumin seeds, and mint into a bowl. Season with salt and pepper and mix well with your hands until thoroughly combined. Shape into walnut-size balls.

3 Heat the remaining oil in a skillet. Add the meatballs and cook over medium heat, turning occasionally, for 6–8 minutes, until evenly browned and cooked through. Remove from the pan and drain on paper towels.

4 Remove the rice mixture from the heat and stir in the butter, then gently stir in the meatballs. Transfer to a warmed serving dish, garnish with cilantro sprigs, and serve immediately.

beef & squash baked with rice

ingredients

serves 4

1 onion, finely chopped
1 pound ground chuck beef
1 tablespoon finely chopped
    fresh mint
½ teaspoon ground cinnamon
1½ sticks butter, plus extra
    for greasing
1¼ cups long-grain rice
1 butternut squash, peeled,
    seeded, and cut into cubes,
    or 1 cup fresh pumpkin cubes
2 tablespoons packed brown sugar
salt and pepper

method

1 Put the onion, beef, mint, and cinnamon into a bowl, season with salt and pepper, and mix well until thoroughly combined. Divide the mixture into eight equal portions and shape into small patties.

2 Melt 4 tablespoons of the butter in a skillet. Add the patties, in batches if necessary, and cook for 3–4 minutes on each side, until lightly browned. Remove with a spatula.

3 Preheat the oven to 375°F. Grease a large casserole dish with butter. Cook the rice in a large saucepan of salted boiling water, according to the package directions, until tender. Drain well and rinse with boiling water.

4 Spoon half the rice into the prepared casserole dish. Melt the remaining butter and pour half of it over the rice. Put the beef patties on top and cover with the remaining rice. Spread the squash cubes over the top, sprinkle with the sugar, and pour the remaining melted butter over the top. Cover and bake in the preheated oven for 25–30 minutes, until the squash is tender. Serve immediately.

beef fried rice

ingredients

serves 6

2¾ cups long-grain rice
2 tablespoons peanut oil
4 extra-large eggs, lightly beaten
1½ pounds ground sirloin beef
1 large onion, finely chopped
2 garlic cloves, finely chopped
1 cup frozen peas
3 tablespoons light soy sauce
1 teaspoon sugar
salt
shrimp crackers, to serve (optional)

method

1 Cook the rice in a large saucepan of salted boiling water, according to the package directions, until tender. Drain the rice, rinse with boiling water, and set aside.

2 Heat a wok over medium heat, then add the peanut oil, swirl it around the wok, and heat. Add the eggs and cook, stirring continuously, for 50–60 seconds, until set. Transfer to a dish and set aside.

3 Add the beef to the wok and stir-fry, breaking it up with a wooden spoon, for 4–5 minutes, until evenly browned. Stir in the onion, garlic, and peas and stir-fry for an additional 3–4 minutes.

4 Add the rice, soy sauce, sugar, and eggs and cook, stirring continuously, for an additional 1–2 minutes, until heated through. Serve the stir-fry immediately with shrimp crackers, if using.

ground beef stroganoff

ingredients

serves 4

3 tablespoons sunflower oil
1 onion, chopped
2 garlic cloves, finely chopped
3 cups sliced white button
    mushrooms
1 pound fresh ground sirloin beef
2 tablespoons brandy
²⁄₃ cup beef stock
²⁄₃ cup sour cream
2 tablespoons chopped fresh
    parsley, plus extra to garnish
salt and pepper
cooked rice, to serve

method

1 Heat 2 tablespoons of the oil in a large skillet. Add the onion and garlic and cook over low heat, stirring occasionally, for 5 minutes, until softened. Add the mushrooms and cook, stirring frequently, for an additional 5 minutes. Using a slotted spoon, transfer the vegetables to a plate.

2 Add the remaining oil to the skillet, then add the beef and cook over medium heat, stirring frequently and breaking it up with a wooden spoon, for 5–8 minutes, until evenly browned. Drain off as much fat as possible.

3 Reduce the heat to low, return the vegetables to the skillet, and stir in the brandy. Cook, stirring occasionally, for 4–5 minutes, until the alcohol has evaporated. Stir in the stock, season with salt and pepper, and simmer gently, stirring frequently, for 15 minutes.

4 Stir in the sour cream and parsley and cook for an additional minute. Garnish with parsley and serve the stroganoff immediately with rice.

chicken, prosciutto & sun-dried tomato mini meatballs

ingredients

serves 4–6

1 pound ground chicken

2 ounces prosciutto, coarsely chopped

3 tablespoons finely chopped fresh flat-leaf parsley

1 egg, beaten

2 cups fresh bread crumbs

1 onion, finely chopped

1 cup finely chopped sun-dried tomatoes

2–3 tablespoons vegetable oil

salt and pepper

tomato sauce and cooked pasta, to serve

method

1 Put the ground chicken, prosciutto, parsley, egg, bread crumbs, onion, tomatoes, and salt and pepper into a large bowl and mix with your fingertips to combine.

2 Shape the mixture into about 30 small balls, place on a baking sheet, and chill for 30 minutes.

3 Heat half the oil in a large, nonstick skillet, add half the meatballs, and cook for 15–20 minutes, turning regularly, until the chicken is thoroughly cooked. Drain the meatballs on paper towels. Repeat with the remaining oil and meatballs.

4 Add to a hot tomato sauce and serve with pasta.

turkey tetrazzini

ingredients

serves 4

2 tablespoons vegetable oil
1 pound ground turkey
1 onion, finely chopped
1 garlic clove, finely chopped
2 celery stalks, finely chopped
3 cups finely sliced white button
　mushrooms
2 tablespoons all-purpose flour
1 cup chicken stock
¼ cup light cream
3–4 drops Worcestershire sauce
1 cup frozen peas
8 ounces dried spaghetti, cooked
　according to package directions
¼ cup freshly grated Parmesan
　cheese
salt and pepper

method

1 Preheat the oven to 400°F. Heat 1 tablespoon of the oil in a large, nonstick skillet, then add the turkey and cook for 4–5 minutes, stirring occasionally until the meat is brown. Remove from the skillet.

2 Heat the remaining oil in the skillet, then add the onion, garlic, celery, and mushrooms and cook for 2–3 minutes, until soft.

3 Add the flour and cook over medium heat, stirring continuously, for 1 minute. Gradually add the stock and bring to a boil, stirring continuously. Stir in the cream, Worcestershire sauce, and peas, then add the turkey and season with salt and pepper. Let simmer for 1–2 minutes.

4 Place the spaghetti in a shallow ovenproof dish, pour the sauce over the pasta, and toss to combine well.

5 Sprinkle with the cheese and bake in the preheated oven for 15–20 minutes, until golden and piping hot. Serve immediately.

sicilian linguine

ingredients

serves 4

½ cup olive oil, plus extra
    for brushing
2 eggplants, sliced
12 ounces ground round beef
1 onion, chopped
2 garlic cloves, finely chopped
2 tablespoons tomato paste
1 (14½-ounce) can diced tomatoes
1 teaspoon Worcestershire sauce
1 tablespoon chopped fresh
    flat-leaf parsley
½ cup pitted ripe black olives,
    sliced
1 red bell pepper, seeded
    and chopped
6 ounces dried linguine
1⅓ cups freshly grated
    Parmesan cheese
salt and pepper

method

1 Preheat the oven to 400°F. Brush an 8-inch springform round cake pan with oil and line the bottom with parchment paper. Heat half the oil in a skillet. Add the eggplant, in batches, and cook until lightly browned on both sides. Add more oil as required. Drain the eggplant on paper towels, then arrange in overlapping slices to cover the bottom and sides of the cake pan, reserving sufficient slices to cover the top.

2 Heat the remaining oil in a large saucepan and add the beef, onion, and garlic. Cook over medium heat, breaking up the meat with a wooden spoon, until browned all over. Add the tomato paste, tomatoes, Worcestershire sauce, and parsley. Season with salt and pepper and simmer for 10 minutes. Add the olives and red bell pepper and cook for an additional 10 minutes.

3 Meanwhile, bring a saucepan of lightly salted water to a boil. Add the pasta, return to a boil, and cook according to the package directions, until tender but still firm to the bite. Drain and transfer to a bowl. Add the meat sauce and Parmesan to the bowl and toss, then spoon into the cake pan, press down, and cover with the remaining eggplant slices. Bake in the preheated oven for 40 minutes. Let stand for 5 minutes, then loosen around the edges and invert onto a plate. Remove and discard the parchment paper and serve.

greek baked pasta

ingredients

serves 6

¼ cup olive oil, plus extra
    for brushing
1 pound fresh ground round beef
1 small onion, finely chopped
2 garlic cloves, finely chopped
2 cups tomato paste
1 teaspoon sugar
2 teaspoons red wine vinegar
3 tablespoons chopped fresh
    flat-leaf parsley
8 ounces dried macaroni
2 cups shredded Swiss cheese
2 eggplants, sliced lengthwise
2 eggs, lightly beaten
1 cup freshly grated Parmesan
    cheese
salt and pepper

white sauce

2½ cups milk
4 tablespoons butter
½ cup all-purpose flour

method

1 Heat half the oil in a saucepan and add the beef, onion, and garlic. Cook over medium heat, breaking up the meat with a wooden spoon, until browned all over. Stir in the tomato paste, sugar, vinegar, and parsley and season with salt and pepper. Reduce the heat, cover, and simmer for 15 minutes, until thickened.

2 Meanwhile, preheat the oven to 350°F. Bring a large saucepan of salted water to a boil. Add the macaroni, return to a boil, and cook for 8–10 minutes, until tender but still firm to the bite. Drain and return to the pan. Stir in the remaining oil and the Swiss cheese.

3 Preheat the broiler to medium–high. Brush a large ovenproof dish with oil. Spread out the eggplant slices on a baking sheet and brush on both sides with oil. Cook under the broiler for 5 minutes on each side, until golden. Line the bottom and sides of the dish with the eggplant.

4 To make the white sauce, heat the milk, butter, and flour in a saucepan, beating continuously, until smooth and thick. Stir in the eggs and Parmesan. Spoon half the macaroni over the eggplant and pour in half the white sauce. Add the beef mixture and top with the remaining macaroni. Pour the remaining sauce over the top. Bake in the preheated oven for 35–40 minutes, until golden brown. Let stand for 10 minutes before serving.

pasta with aromatic beef sauce

ingredients

serves 4

2 tablespoons sunflower oil
4 shallots, finely chopped
1 garlic clove, finely chopped
1 pound ground sirloin beef
3 tablespoons red wine
1½ cups chopped white button
    mushrooms
½ teaspoon ground cinnamon
½ teaspoon ground allspice
1 tablespoon chopped
    fresh parsley
1 fresh basil sprig, leaves torn,
    plus extra sprigs to garnish
1 (14½-ounce) can diced tomatoes
2 tablespoons ketchup
12 ounces dried conchiglie
    or other pasta shapes
salt and pepper

method

1 Heat the oil in a skillet. Add the shallots and garlic and cook over low heat, stirring occasionally, for 5 minutes, until softened. Add the beef, increase the heat to medium, and cook, stirring frequently and breaking it up with a wooden spoon, for 8–10 minutes, until browned all over. Drain off as much fat as possible.

2 Stir in the wine and simmer over low heat, stirring frequently, for 5 minutes. Add the mushrooms, cinnamon, allspice, parsley, torn basil, tomatoes, and ketchup, then season with salt and pepper and mix well. Cover and simmer over low heat, stirring occasionally, for 1 hour. If the mixture seems to be drying out, add a little water.

3 Meanwhile, bring a large saucepan of salted water to a boil. Add the pasta, return to a boil, and cook according to the package directions, until tender but still firm to the bite. Drain and toss with the beef sauce. Garnish with basil sprigs and serve immediately.

one-dish pasta

ingredients

serves 4

2 tablespoons olive oil
1 onion, chopped
1 garlic clove, finely chopped
1 celery stalk, chopped
1 carrot, chopped
1 pound ground sirloin beef
2 cups sliced white button
    mushrooms
1 (14½-ounce) can diced tomatoes
1 tablespoon tomato paste
1 teaspoon sugar
pinch of dried oregano
1 tablespoon chopped fresh
    flat-leaf parsley
6 ounces dried fusilli
    (corkscrew pasta)
¾ cup red wine
1½ tablespoons concentrated beef
    stock or 1 beef bouillon cube
salt and pepper

method

1 Heat the oil in a large saucepan with a tight-fitting lid. Add the onion, garlic, celery, and carrot and cook over low heat, stirring occasionally, for 5 minutes, until softened. Add the beef, increase the heat to medium, and cook, stirring frequently and breaking up the meat with a wooden spoon, for 5–8 minutes, until evenly browned.

2 Add the mushrooms and cook for an additional 3–4 minutes. Add the tomatoes, tomato paste, sugar, herbs, pasta, and wine. Stir in the concentrated stock, add just enough water to cover, and stir well.

3 Reduce the heat, cover tightly, and simmer gently for 15–20 minutes, until the pasta is tender but still firm to the bite and the sauce has thickened. Season with salt and pepper and serve immediately.

spaghetti with meat sauce

ingredients

serves 4

12 ounces dried spaghetti
fresh Parmesan cheese shavings,
    to garnish (optional)
fresh thyme sprigs, to garnish
crusty bread, to serve

meat sauce

2 tablespoons olive oil
1 onion, finely chopped
2 garlic cloves, finely chopped
1 carrot, finely chopped
1 cup sliced or chopped white
    button mushrooms (optional)
1 teaspoon dried oregano
½ teaspoon dried thyme
1 bay leaf
10 ounces ground sirloin beef
1¼ cups stock
1¼ cups tomato paste
salt and pepper

method

1 To make the sauce, heat the oil in a heavy, nonstick saucepan. Add the onion and cook, half covered, for 5 minutes, or until soft. Add the garlic, carrot, and mushrooms, if using, and cook for an additional 3 minutes, stirring occasionally.

2 Add the herbs and beef to the pan and cook until the meat has browned, stirring regularly.

3 Add the stock and tomato paste. Reduce the heat, season with salt and pepper, and cook over medium–low heat, half covered, for 15–20 minutes, or until the sauce has reduced and thickened. Remove and discard the bay leaf.

4 Meanwhile, bring a large saucepan of lightly salted water to a boil. Add the pasta, return to a boil, and cook according to the package directions, until tender but still firm to the bite. Drain well and mix together the pasta and sauce until the pasta is well coated. Serve immediately with crusty bread and garnished with Parmesan cheese shavings, if using, and thyme sprigs.

meatballs in tomato sauce

ingredients

serves 4

3 slices white bread,
    crusts removed
1½ pounds ground chuck beef
1 onion, finely chopped
½ cup ketchup
1 egg, lightly beaten
3 tablespoons water
salt and pepper
chopped fresh parsley,
    to garnish

tomato sauce

2 tablespoons sunflower oil
1 onion, finely chopped
2 garlic cloves, finely chopped
2 tablespoons tomato paste
½ cup water
1 (14½-ounce) can diced tomatoes
1–2 teaspoons packed light
    brown sugar

method

1 Tear the bread into pieces, put it into a bowl, and pour in enough water to cover. Let soak for 5 minutes.

2 Put the beef, onion, ketchup, and egg into a bowl and season with salt and pepper. Squeeze out the bread, add it to the bowl, and mix well with your hands until thoroughly combined and smooth. Add the 3 tablespoons of water and knead for 5 minutes. Set aside while you make the sauce.

3 For the tomato sauce, heat the oil in a saucepan. Add the onion and garlic and cook over low heat, stirring occasionally, for 5 minutes, until softened. Meanwhile, mix the tomato paste with the ½ cup of water in a small bowl. Add to the saucepan with the tomatoes and bring to a boil, then reduce the heat and simmer, stirring occasionally, for 15–20 minutes, until thickened. Transfer the sauce to a food processor or blender and process to a puree. Pour into a clean pan and stir in the sugar to taste.

4 Meanwhile, shape the beef mixture into 20 small meatballs, rolling them between the palms of your hands. Bring the sauce back to a simmer, then add the meatballs and simmer gently, occasionally shaking the pan, for 30 minutes, until cooked through. Transfer to a serving dish, garnish with parsley, and serve immediately.

chicken meatball pasta

ingredients

serves 4

3 tablespoons olive oil
1 red onion, chopped
1 pound ground chicken
1 cup fresh white bread crumbs
2 teaspoons dried oregano
1 garlic clove, crushed
1 (14½-ounce) can diced tomatoes
1 tablespoon tomato paste
1¼ cups water
8 ounces dried linguine
salt and pepper
Parmesan cheese shavings,
    to serve

method

1 Heat 1 tablespoon of the oil in a large skillet and sauté half the chopped onion for 5 minutes, until just softened. Let cool.

2 Place the chicken, bread crumbs, oregano, and sautéed onion in a food processor or blender. Season well with salt and pepper and process for 2–3 minutes, until thoroughly combined. Shape into 24 meatballs.

3 Heat the remaining oil in the skillet and cook the meatballs over medium–high heat for 3–4 minutes, until golden brown. Remove and set aside.

4 Add the remaining onion and the garlic to the skillet and sauté for 5 minutes. Stir in the tomatoes, tomato paste, and water, and bring to a boil. Add the meatballs, reduce the heat and simmer for 20 minutes. Season with salt and pepper.

5 Meanwhile, bring a large saucepan of lightly salted water to a boil. Add the pasta, return to a boil, and cook according to the package directions, until tender but still firm to the bite. Drain the pasta well and toss with the meatballs and sauce. Serve immediately with Parmesan cheese shavings.

penne with turkey meatballs

ingredients

serves 4

12 ounces ground turkey
1 small garlic clove, finely chopped
2 tablespoons finely chopped
    fresh parsley
1 egg, lightly beaten
all-purpose flour, for dusting
3 tablespoons olive oil
1 onion, finely chopped
1 celery stalk, finely chopped
1 carrot, finely chopped
1¾ cups tomato paste
1 fresh rosemary sprig
1 bay leaf
12 ounces dried penne
salt and pepper
freshly grated Parmesan cheese,
    to serve

method

1 Put the turkey, garlic, and parsley in a bowl and mix well. Stir in the egg and season with salt and pepper. Dust your hands lightly with flour and shape the mixture into walnut-size balls between your palms. Lightly dust each meatball with flour.

2 Heat the oil in a saucepan. Add the onion, celery, and carrot and cook over low heat, stirring occasionally, for 5 minutes, until softened. Increase the heat to medium, add the meatballs, and cook, turning frequently, for 8–10 minutes, until golden brown all over.

3 Pour in the tomato paste, add the rosemary and bay leaf, season with salt and pepper, and bring to a boil. Reduce the heat, cover, and simmer gently, stirring occasionally, for 40–45 minutes. Remove and discard the herbs.

4 Shortly before the meatballs are ready, bring a large saucepan of lightly salted water to a boil. Add the pasta, return to a boil, and cook according to the package directions, until tender but still firm to the bite. Drain and add to the pan with the meatballs. Stir gently and heat through briefly, then spoon into individual warm dishes. Sprinkle with Parmesan cheese and serve immediately

one-dish chili & rice

ingredients

serves 4

1 pound ground sirloin beef
1 large onion, finely chopped
2 garlic cloves, finely chopped
1 red bell pepper, seeded and
    finely chopped
2 celery stalks, finely chopped
2 teaspoons hot chili powder
1 teaspoon cumin seeds
2 tablespoons tomato paste
1¼ cups brown long-grain rice
1 (14½-ounce) can diced tomatoes
2 teaspoons unsweetened
    cocoa powder
2½ cups beef stock
1 (15-ounce) can black beans,
    drained and rinsed
salt and pepper
sour cream and nachos, to serve

method

1 Dry-fry the beef in a large, deep, flameproof casserole
dish or saucepan for 4–5 minutes, until starting to
brown. Add the onion, garlic, red bell pepper, and
celery and continue cooking for an additional
2–3 minutes, stirring continuously. Add the chili
powder and cumin seeds and cook for 1–2 minutes.

2 Add the tomato paste and cook for an additional
1 minute, stirring continuously. Stir in the rice, tomatoes,
cocoa powder, and stock, season with salt and pepper,
then cover and cook for 20 minutes, stirring occasionally.

3 Stir in the beans and continue to cook for an additional
10 minutes, until the rice is fully cooked. Serve with
sour cream to drizzle on top and with the nachos
on the side.

chinese noodles with beef & shredded vegetables

ingredients

serves 4

1 pound dried egg noodles
3 tablespoons peanut oil
3 scallions, thinly sliced
2 garlic cloves, finely chopped
$\frac{1}{2}$-inch piece fresh ginger,
    finely chopped
12 ounces ground sirloin beef
1 tablespoon sesame oil
$\frac{1}{3}$ cup soy sauce
2 tablespoons Chinese rice wine
    or dry sherry
1 tablespoon sugar
1 tablespoon cornstarch
$\frac{1}{4}$ cup water
salt

to serve

1 cup fresh bean sprouts, blanched
4 ounces Chinese greens,
    blanched and shredded
2 carrots, blanched and shredded
1 cup shredded cucumber
1 cup shredded radishes

method

1 Put the bean sprouts and shredded vegetables into small serving dishes and set aside. Cook the noodles in a large saucepan of salted boiling water according to the package directions, then drain and keep warm.

2 Meanwhile, heat a wok or skillet over medium heat, then add the peanut oil and swirl it around the pan to heat. Add the scallions, garlic, and ginger and stir-fry for 2 minutes. Add the beef and stir-fry, breaking it up with a wooden spoon, for 5 minutes, until evenly browned. Stir in the sesame oil, soy sauce, rice wine, and sugar and cook, stirring continuously, for an additional 3 minutes.

3 Mix the cornstarch to a paste with the water in a small bowl and add to the wok. Simmer, stirring continuously, until the sauce has thickened and become glossy.

4 Divide the noodles among individual warm bowls and top with the beef mixture and shredded vegetables. Serve immediately.

chinese-style fried rice

ingredients

serves 4

2 tablespoons vegetable oil
4 eggs, beaten
8 ounces ground chicken
1 bunch scallions, trimmed and
    finely chopped
2 garlic cloves, finely chopped
2 teaspoons Chinese five-spice
    powder
2 cups long-grain rice, cooked,
    cooled, and chilled
4 ounces shrimp, cooked
1 cup frozen peas
⅔ cup drained canned corn kernels
1 cup finely chopped fresh cilantro
1 teaspoon toasted sesame oil
salt and pepper

method

1 Heat 1 tablespoon of the vegetable oil in a wok or large, nonstick skillet. Season the eggs with salt and pepper, then add to the wok and gently whisk with a fork until lightly cooked. Remove from the wok and coarsely chop. Wipe out the wok with paper towels.

2 Heat the remaining oil in the wok, add the ground chicken, and cook for 4–5 minutes, until it is brown and crumbles.

3 Add the scallions, garlic, and five-spice powder and cook for an additional 1–2 minutes, stirring continuously.

4 Add the rice, shrimp, peas, corn kernels, and half the cilantro. Stir-fry until everything is piping hot.

5 Stir in the cooked egg and sesame oil, season with salt and pepper, sprinkle with the remaining cilantro, and serve immediately.

variation

Use 8 ounces ground pork instead of chicken, 2 ounces shiitake mushrooms instead of the corn kernels, and omit the cooked shrimp.

burgers & kabobs

classic cheeseburgers

ingredients

serves 4

1¾ pounds ground chuck beef
1 beef bouillon cube
1 tablespoon ground dried onion
2 tablespoons water
1–2 tablespoons sunflower oil
4 slices American, Swiss, or
   cheddar cheese

to serve

lettuce leaves
4 hamburger buns, halved
beefsteak tomato slices
fries

method

1 Place the beef in a large mixing bowl. Crumble the bouillon cube over the meat, add the dried onion and water, and mix well. Divide the meat into four portions, shape each into a ball, then flatten slightly to make a patty of your preferred thickness.

2 Place a ridged grill pan over medium–high heat. Lightly brush the burgers with oil and cook for 5–6 minutes. Turn the burgers, place a slice of the cheese on top of the cooked side, and cook for an additional 5–6 minutes, until thoroughly cooked.

3 Place the lettuce leaves on the bottom halves of the buns and top with the burgers. Place a couple of tomato slices on top and add the lids. Serve immediately with fries.

cheese-stuffed burgers

ingredients

serves 4

1 pound ground chuck beef
1 onion, finely chopped
1 garlic clove, finely chopped
1 teaspoon creamed horseradish
1 tablespoon chopped fresh thyme
⅓ cup crumbled blue cheese or feta
　　cheese
4 hamburger buns, halved
　　and toasted
salt and pepper
arugula leaves, to serve

method

1 Preheat the broiler to medium–high and line the pan beneath the rack with aluminum foil. Put the beef, onion, garlic, horseradish, and thyme into a bowl. Season with salt and pepper and mix well until thoroughly combined. Divide the mixture into eight portions and shape each portion into a patty shape.

2 Sprinkle the cheese over four of the patties and top with the remaining patties. Gently press together the edges, smoothing them with a frosting spatula to enclose the cheese completely.

3 Cook under the preheated broiler for 5–6 minutes on each side, turning them carefully with a spatula. Serve in the toasted buns with arugula leaves.

cheese & apple burgers

ingredients

serves 4

1 pound ground chuck beef
1 onion, finely chopped
1–2 teaspoons whole-grain
    mustard, or to taste
2–3 teaspoons Worcestershire
    sauce
½ cup shredded sharp
    cheddar cheese
2 Granny Smith apples
1 teaspoon butter, melted
2–3 teaspoons sugar
4 slices Swiss cheese
4 hamburger buns, halved
    and toasted
salt and pepper
spinach leaves, to serve

method

1 Place the ground beef in a large bowl and add the onion and mustard. Season with salt, pepper, and Worcestershire sauce, and add the cheddar cheese. Peel and core one of the apples, then grate and add to the bowl. Mix together, then shape into four even burgers. Cover and let chill for 30 minutes.

2 Preheat the broiler to medium–high and line a broiler rack with aluminum foil. Peel and core the remaining apple, then cut into 4–6 thick slices. Brush with the melted butter and sprinkle with the sugar. Place on the prepared broiler rack and cook under the hot broiler for 2–3 minutes on each side, or until caramelized. Reserve.

3 Cook the burgers under the preheated broiler for 4–6 minutes on each side, until thoroughly cooked. Top the burgers with the sliced cheese and broil until the cheese has melted. Serve in the toasted buns with fresh spinach leaves and the caramelized apple slices.

variation

Use 1 pound lean ground pork instead of ground beef.

blt burgers with asparagus

ingredients

serves 4–6

8 ounces bacon strips, any rind
    removed and finely chopped
1 pound ground round beef
1 onion, grated
2–4 garlic cloves, crushed
salt and pepper

dip

6 ounces baby asparagus spears
1 tablespoon lemon juice
1 small ripe avocado, peeled,
    pitted, and finely chopped
2 firm tomatoes, peeled, seeded,
    and finely chopped
$^2/_3$ cup sour cream

to serve

lettuce leaves
hamburger buns, halved
beefsteak tomato slices

method

1 Place the bacon, ground beef, onion, garlic, and salt and pepper in a large bowl and mix well. Shape into 4–6 even patties, then cover and let chill in the refrigerator for 30 minutes.

2 To make the dip, trim the asparagus and cook in a saucepan of lightly salted boiling water for 5 minutes, then drain and plunge into cold water. When cold, drain and finely chop half the spears into a bowl and reserve the rest to serve. Sprinkle the lemon juice over the avocado. Stir the avocado, tomatoes, and sour cream into the chopped asparagus. Season with salt and pepper, cover, and let chill until required.

3 Preheat the broiler to medium–high and line the pan beneath the rack with aluminum foil. Place the patties on the prepared broiler rack and cook under the preheated broiler for 3–5 minutes on each side, or until they are thoroughly cooked.

4 Place the lettuce leaves on the bottom halves of the burger buns and top with the burgers. Top with a tomato slice, an asparagus spear, and a spoonful of the dip. Add the lids and serve immediately.

italian cheese burgers

ingredients

serves 4

1 pound ground chuck beef
1 onion, grated
2–4 garlic cloves, crushed
1 small red bell pepper, seeded,
    peeled, and chopped
½ cup finely chopped, pitted
    ripe black olives
1 tablespoon tomato paste
2 large tomatoes, thickly sliced
4 slices Swiss cheese
pepper
4 hamburger buns, halved
    and toasted
salad greens, to serve

method

1 Place the ground beef, onion, garlic, red bell pepper, olives, pepper, and tomato paste in a food processor or blender and, using the pulse button, blend together. Shape into four even patties, then cover and let chill for at least 30 minutes.

2 Preheat the broiler to medium–high and line the pan beneath the rack with aluminum foil. Place the patties on the prepared broiler rack and cook under the preheated broiler for 3–5 minutes on each side, until thoroughly cooked.

3 Place tomato slices on top of each burger, then place the cheese over the tomato. Broil for an additional 2–3 minutes, or until the cheese begins to melt. Serve in the toasted buns with salad greens.

beef & beet burgers

ingredients

serves 4

3 tablespoons sunflower oil
1 onion, finely chopped
1½ pounds ground chuck beef
1 medium egg, lightly beaten
2 teaspoons white wine vinegar
½ teaspoon paprika
1 tablespoon finely chopped
   drained capers
3 tablespoons finely chopped
   cooked beet
2 tablespoons sour cream
4 tablespoons butter
4 eggs
salt and pepper

method

1 Heat 1 tablespoon of the oil in a skillet. Add the onion and cook over low heat, stirring occasionally, for 5 minutes, until softened.

2 Transfer the onion to a large bowl and add the beef, egg, vinegar, paprika, and capers and mix well with your hands. Add the beet and sour cream, season with salt and pepper, and mix well again. Shape the mixture into four patties.

3 Melt 2 tablespoons of the butter with the remaining oil in a skillet. Add the patties and cook over medium heat for 6–7 minutes on each side, until well browned. Remove with a spatula and drain on paper towels.

4 Melt half the remaining butter in a skillet. Break two of the eggs into separate cups and slide them into the skillet. Immediately collect the whites around the yolks with a slotted spoon to keep them neat and separated and cook for a few minutes until the whites have set but the yolks are still runny; keep warm. Cook the remaining eggs in the remaining butter in the same way. Transfer the burgers to a warm serving dish, top with the fried eggs, and serve immediately.

beef & bacon burgers

ingredients

serves 6

1½ pounds ground chuck beef
1 large onion, finely chopped
1 garlic clove, finely chopped
    (optional)
2 cups fresh bread crumbs
2 teaspoons chopped fresh sage
1 extra-large egg, lightly beaten
6 bacon slices
3 tablespoons butter, melted
salt and pepper

method

1 Preheat the broiler to medium–high and line the broiler rack with aluminum foil. Put the beef, onion, garlic (if using), bread crumbs, sage, and egg into a bowl, season with salt and pepper, and mix well until thoroughly combined. Divide the mixture into six even portions and shape into balls, then gently flatten into patties.

2 Wrap a bacon slice around each patty and secure with a wooden toothpick.

3 Brush one side of each patty with a little of the melted butter and cook under the preheated broiler for 5 minutes. Carefully turn the burgers with a spatula, brush with the remaining melted butter, and broil for an additional 4–5 minutes, until thoroughly cooked.

4 Remove and discard the toothpicks. Serve immediately.

chili burgers with cilantro & scallions

ingredients

serves 4

¾ cup drained, rinsed canned
 red kidney beans
1 pound ground chuck beef
1–2 fresh red chiles, seeded
 and chopped
2–4 garlic cloves, crushed
6 scallions, chopped
1 tablespoon chopped fresh
 cilantro
4 taco shells
shredded lettuce
shredded carrot
salt and pepper
sour cream, to serve

salsa

3 ripe tomatoes, peeled and
 finely chopped
1 small ripe avocado, peeled,
 pitted, and mashed
4 scallions, finely chopped
1 fresh red chile, seeded and finely
 chopped
1 tablespoon chopped fresh
cilantro

method

1 Place the kidney beans in a food processor and blend for 1 minute.

2 Add the ground beef, chiles, garlic, scallions, and cilantro to the food processor, season with salt and pepper, and blend for 2 minutes. Shape into four even patties, then cover and let chill for 30 minutes.

3 Meanwhile, make the salsa. Mix together the tomatoes, avocado, scallions, chile, and cilantro. Place in a small bowl, cover, and let stand for at least 30 minutes to let the flavors develop.

4 Heat a nonstick skillet until hot. When hot, add the patties and cook over medium heat for 3–5 minutes on each side, until thoroughly cooked.

5 Heat the taco shells according to the package directions and fill with the shredded lettuce and carrot. Serve alongside the burgers, topped with the salsa and sour cream to serve.

sloppy joes

ingredients

serves 4–6

1½ pounds ground chuck beef
½ onion, diced
2 garlic cloves, finely chopped
1 green bell pepper, seeded
    and diced
2 cups water
¾ cup ketchup
1½ tablespoons packed light
    brown sugar
dash of Worcestershire sauce
1 teaspoon Dijon mustard
1½ teaspoons salt
½ teaspoon black pepper
cayenne pepper
hamburger buns, halved

method

1 Put the beef and onion into a large, cold skillet and place over medium heat. Cook, stirring, breaking up the meat into small pieces with a wooden spoon, until it begins to brown.

2 Add the garlic and green bell pepper and cook, stirring, for 2 minutes. Add half the water. Cook until simmering, scraping up any sediment from the bottom of the skillet.

3 Stir in the ketchup, sugar, Worcestershire sauce, mustard, salt, black pepper, cayenne pepper, and the remaining water. Bring to simmering point, reduce the heat to low, and simmer for 30–45 minutes, or until most of the liquid has evaporated and the meat mixture is thick, rich, and tender. Spoon the beef mixture onto each bun bottom. Add the bun lids and serve immediately.

bacon-wrapped chicken burgers

ingredients

serves 4

1 pound ground chicken
1 onion, finely chopped
2 garlic cloves, crushed
½ cup pine nuts, toasted
½ cup shredded Swiss cheese
2 tablespoons fresh snipped chives
2 tablespoons whole-wheat flour
8 bacon strips
1–2 tablespoons sunflower oil
salt and pepper

to serve

crusty rolls, split
red onion slices
lettuce leaves
mayonnaise
scallions, chopped

method

1 Place the ground chicken, onion, garlic, pine nuts, Swiss cheese, chives, and salt and pepper in a food processor or blender. Using the pulse button, blend together the mixture using short, sharp bursts. Scrape out onto a board and shape into four even patties. Coat in the flour, then cover and chill for 1 hour.

2 Wrap each patty with two bacon strips, securing in place with a wooden toothpick.

3 Heat a heavy skillet and add the oil. When hot, add the patties and cook over medium heat for 5–6 minutes on each side, or until thoroughly cooked.

4 Remove and discard the toothpicks. Serve the burgers in the crusty rolls with the red onion, lettuce, a spoonful of mayonnaise, and scallions. Serve immediately.

turkey & tarragon burgers

ingredients

serves 4

⅓ cup bulgur wheat
1 pound ground turkey
1 tablespoon finely grated
    orange rind
1 red onion, finely chopped
1 yellow bell pepper, seeded,
    peeled, and finely chopped
¼ cup toasted slivered almonds
1 tablespoon chopped fresh
    tarragon
salt and pepper

to serve
lettuce leaves
tomato and onion salad

method

1 Cook the bulgur wheat in a saucepan of lightly salted boiling water according to the package directions.

2 Drain the bulgur wheat and place in a bowl with the ground turkey, orange rind, onion, yellow bell pepper, almonds, tarragon, and salt and pepper. Mix together, then shape into four even patties. Cover and let chill in the refrigerator for 1 hour.

3 Preheat the broiler to medium–high and line the pan beneath the rack with aluminum foil. Place the patties on the prepared broiler rack and cook under the preheated broiler for 3–5 minutes on each side, until thoroughly cooked.

4 Put a few lettuce leaves on serving plates and place a burger on top of each. Serve immediately with a tomato and onion salad.

turkey & bean burgers

ingredients

serves 6

¾ cup drained, rinsed canned
    red kidney beans
½ bunch scallions, trimmed
    and finely chopped
1 garlic clove, crushed
1 pound ground turkey
¼ cup sweet chili sauce
pinch of crushed red pepper
vegetable oil, for frying
salt and pepper

to serve

toasted ciabatta rolls
fresh arugula leaves
beefsteak tomato slices

method

1 Place the beans in a mixing bowl and crush with the back of a fork. Add the scallions, garlic, ground turkey, chili sauce, crushed red pepper, and salt and pepper. Use your fingertips to combine.

2 Shape the mixture into six patty shapes. Heat the oil in a skillet, add the burgers, and cook for 6–7 minutes on each side, until thoroughly cooked.

3 Serve immediately in toasted ciabatta rolls with arugula leaves and sliced tomatoes.

maple-glazed turkey burgers

ingredients

serves 4

2 fresh ears of corn (in their husks)
1 pound ground turkey
1 red bell pepper, seeded
    and finely chopped
6 scallions, finely chopped
1 cup fresh white bread crumbs
2 tablespoons chopped fresh basil
2 tablespoons maple syrup
salt and pepper

to serve

arugula leaves
beefsteak tomato slices
cheese-topped hamburger buns,
    halved
corn relish

method

1 Heat a ridged grill pan until hot, then add the ears of corn and cook over medium–high heat, turning occasionally, for 8–10 minutes, or until the husks are charred. Remove from the pan and let cool, then strip off the husks and silks. Using a sharp knife, cut away the kernels and place in a bowl.

2 Add the ground turkey, red bell pepper, scallions, bread crumbs, and basil to the corn kernels in the bowl. Season with salt and pepper. Mix together, then shape into four even patties. Cover and let chill in the refrigerator for 1 hour.

3 Preheat the broiler to medium–high and line the pan beneath the rack with aluminum foil. Place the patties on the prepared broiler rack, brush with maple syrup, and cook under the preheated broiler for 3–5 minutes on each side, until thoroughly cooked.

4 Place the arugula and tomato slices on the bottom halves of the buns and top with the burgers. Spoon a little relish over the burgers, add the lids, and serve immediately.

mexican turkey burgers

ingredients

serves 4

1 pound ground turkey
1 cup canned refried beans
2–4 garlic cloves, crushed
1–2 fresh jalapeño chiles, seeded
    and finely chopped
2 tablespoons tomato paste
1 tablespoon chopped fresh
    cilantro
salt and pepper

to serve

shredded baby spinach leaves
4 cheese-topped hamburger buns,
    halved
salsa
guacamole
tortilla chips

method

1 Place the ground turkey in a bowl and break up any large lumps. Beat the refried beans until smooth, then add to the turkey in the bowl.

2 Add the garlic, chiles, tomato paste, and cilantro, season with salt and pepper, and mix together. Shape into four even patties, then cover and let chill in the refrigerator for 1 hour.

3 Preheat the broiler to medium–high and line the broiler rack with aluminum foil. Place the patties on the prepared broiler rack and cook under the hot broiler for 3–5 minutes on each side, or until thoroughly cooked.

4 Place the spinach on the bottom halves of the burger buns and top with the burgers. Spoon a little salsa and guacamole over the burgers and top with the lids. Serve immediately with tortilla chips on the side.

lemon & herb chicken burgers

ingredients

serves 4

8 ounces ground chicken
1 garlic clove, crushed
1 tablespoon honey
finely grated zest of 1 lemon
juice of ½ lemon
1 tablespoon fresh thyme leaves,
    finely chopped
½ bunch scallions, trimmed and
    finely chopped
1–2 tablespoons vegetable oil,
    for frying
salt and pepper

method

1 Put the ground chicken, garlic, honey, lemon zest, lemon juice, thyme, and scallions in a bowl, season with salt and pepper, and use your fingertips to combine. Shape the mixture into four patties, transfer to a plate, cover, and let chill in the refrigerator for at least 30 minutes.

2 Heat the oil in a skillet over medium heat, then add the patties and cook for 5–7 minutes on each side, until the chicken is thoroughly cooked. Serve the burgers immediately.

yakitori-style chicken patties

ingredients

serves 4

8 ounces ground chicken
1 tablespoon grated fresh ginger
1 garlic clove, finely chopped
1 tablespoon ketjap manis or
    2 teaspoons soy sauce and
    1 teaspoon honey
½ bunch scallions, trimmed and
    finely chopped
1–2 tablespoons vegetable oil
fresh mango salsa and noodle
    salad, to serve

method

1 Put the ground chicken, ginger, garlic, ketjap manis, and scallions into a bowl and use your fingertips to combine. Shape the mixture into four patties, transfer to a plate, cover, and let chill for at least 30 minutes.

2 Preheat a ridged grill pan over medium heat, then add the oil. Add the patties and cook for 5–6 minutes on each side, until the chicken is thoroughly cooked. Serve immediately with mango salsa and noodle salad.

beef kabobs

ingredients

serves 6–8

2¼ pounds ground chuck beef
1 Bermuda onion, grated
3 garlic cloves, finely chopped
¼ cup chopped fresh cilantro
1 teaspoon ground cumin
½ teaspoon ground cinnamon
½ teaspoon ground turmeric
1 teaspoon paprika
1 extra-large egg, lightly beaten
3 tablespoons finely chopped fresh
    mint, plus extra leaves to
    garnish
⅔ cup plain yogurt
sunflower oil, for brushing
salt and pepper
lime wedges, to garnish

method

1 Put the beef, onion, garlic, cilantro, and spices into a bowl and season with salt and pepper. Add the egg and mix well with your hands until thoroughly combined and smooth. Cover the bowl with plastic wrap and chill in the refrigerator for 30 minutes. Meanwhile, soak wooden skewers, if using, in water for 30 minutes.

2 Mix together the chopped mint and yogurt in a bowl and season with salt. Cover with plastic wrap and chill until required.

3 Preheat the broiler to medium–high and brush the broiler rack with oil. Remove the beef mixture from the refrigerator, scoop up pieces with your hands, and shape into small ovals about ³/₄ inch thick. Thread the ovals onto metal or presoaked wooden skewers, with three ovals to each skewer.

4 Cook the skewers, in batches if necessary, under the preheated broiler, turning occasionally, for 10–12 minutes, until thoroughly cooked. Garnish with mint leaves and lime wedges and serve immediately with the minted yogurt.

indian kabobs

ingredients

serves 4

1 onion, finely chopped

2 garlic cloves, finely chopped

1½-inch piece fresh ginger,
   finely chopped

2 fresh green chiles, seeded and
   finely chopped

½ teaspoon ground turmeric

2 tablespoons chopped fresh
   cilantro, plus extra to garnish

3 tablespoons plain yogurt,
   plus extra to serve

1 tablespoon lemon juice

1½ pounds ground chuck beef

¼ cup fresh bread crumbs

melted butter, for brushing

salt

tomato and onion salad and
   warm naan, to serve

method

1 Soak 12 wooden skewers, if using, in water to prevent them from charring. Put the onion, garlic, ginger, chiles, turmeric, cilantro, yogurt, lemon juice, beef, and bread crumbs into a bowl. Season with salt and mix well with your hands until thoroughly combined. Cover with plastic wrap and let rest at room temperature for 30 minutes.

2 Preheat the broiler to medium–high. Brush 12 metal or presoaked wooden skewers with melted butter. Dampen your hands and shape the beef mixture into 24 oval shapes. Thread two onto each prepared skewer and place them in the broiler pan.

3 Brush with a little melted butter and cook under the preheated broiler, in batches if necessary, for 5 minutes. Turn the skewers, brush with more melted butter, and cook for an additional 4 minutes, until the kabobs are thoroughly cooked and browned.

4 Transfer the kabobs to a warm serving dish, drizzle with yogurt, and garnish with cilantro. Serve immediately with tomato and onion salad and naan.

casseroles

lasagna with meatballs

ingredients

serves 6

4 tablespoons butter
4 ounces pancetta
1 onion, finely chopped
1 celery stalk, finely chopped
1 carrot, finely chopped
12 ounces ground round beef
⅓ cup red wine
2 tablespoons tomato paste
2 eggs
2 cups freshly grated Parmesan cheese
¾ cup fresh bread crumbs
2 tablespoons olive oil
1½ cups ricotta cheese
8 dried oven-ready lasagna noodles
12 ounces mozzarella cheese, sliced
salt and pepper
chopped fresh parsley, to garnish

method

1 Heat the butter in a large saucepan. Add the pancetta, onion, celery, and carrot and cook over low heat, until soft. Increase the heat to medium, add half the ground beef, and cook until evenly browned. Stir in the wine and tomato paste, season with salt and pepper, and bring to a boil. Reduce the heat, cover, and simmer gently for 1½ hours, until the ground beef is tender.

2 Mix the rest of the ground beef in a bowl with 1 egg, 1 tablespoon of the Parmesan cheese, and the bread crumbs. Shape into walnut-size balls.

3 Heat the oil in a skillet, add the meatballs, and cook for 5–8 minutes, until brown. Pass the ricotta through a strainer into a bowl. Stir in the remaining egg and ¼ cup of the remaining Parmesan cheese.

4 Preheat the oven to 350°F. In a rectangular ovenproof dish, make layers with the lasagna noodles, ricotta mixture, meat sauce, meatballs, and mozzarella cheese. Finish with a layer of the ricotta mixture and sprinkle with the remaining Parmesan cheese. Bake the lasagna in the preheated oven for 20–25 minutes, until golden and bubbling. Serve immediately, garnished with chopped parsley.

beef wrapped in pastry

ingredients

serves 4

butter, for greasing
12 ounces ground round beef
2 onions, finely chopped
1 garlic clove, finely chopped
1 cup fresh bread crumbs
2 Granny Smith apples, peeled,
    cored, and finely chopped
1 tablespoon Dijon mustard
2 tablespoons chopped
    fresh parsley
2 eggs
¼ cup beef stock
1 sheet ready-to-bake puff
    pastry, thawed if frozen
all-purpose flour, for dusting
salt and pepper

method

1 Preheat the oven to 350°F. Grease an 8½-inch loaf pan with butter. Put the beef, onions, garlic, bread crumbs, apples, mustard, and parsley into a bowl and mix well. Beat one of the eggs with the stock and add to the bowl. Season with salt and pepper and mix until combined.

2 Spoon the mixture into the prepared pan. Bake in the preheated oven for 45 minutes. Remove from the oven, and pour off any fat. Let cool completely and invert when cold.

3 Preheat the oven to 425°F. Roll out the pastry on a lightly floured surface to a thickness of about ¼ inch. Put the meatloaf in the center, brush the edges of the pastry with water, and fold over to enclose the meat completely, trimming off any excess pastry. Put the package, seam side down, on a baking sheet. Roll out the trimmings and use to make decorations. Brush with water and arrange on top of the package. Lightly beat the remaining egg and brush it over the package, then make two to three slits in the pastry.

4 Bake in the preheated oven for 35 minutes, until puffed up and golden brown. Reduce the oven temperature to 350°F and bake for an additional 10 minutes. Serve immediately.

meatloaf

ingredients

serves 4

1 pound ground sirloin beef
1 onion, finely chopped
2 garlic cloves, finely chopped
   (optional)
2 cups finely chopped white
   button mushrooms
2 cups fresh bread crumbs
2 eggs, lightly beaten
2 teaspoons Dijon mustard
1 teaspoon Worcestershire sauce
1 teaspoon celery salt
1 tablespoon chopped
   fresh parsley
8–10 bacon strips
pepper

tomato sauce

2 tablespoons sunflower oil
1 onion, finely chopped
2 garlic cloves, finely chopped
2 tablespoons tomato paste
½ cup water
1 (14½-ounce) can diced tomatoes

method

1 Preheat the oven to 325°F. Put the beef, onion, garlic (if using), mushrooms, bread crumbs, eggs, mustard, Worcestershire sauce, celery salt, and parsley into a bowl. Season with pepper and mix well until thoroughly combined.

2 Spoon the mixture into a 9-inch loaf pan, pressing it down well. Cover with the bacon. Put the loaf pan into a roasting pan and pour in boiling water to come about halfway up the sides. Bake in the preheated oven for 1½ hours, until a toothpick inserted into the center comes out clean.

3 Meanwhile, make the tomato sauce. Heat the oil in a saucepan, add the onion and garlic, and cook over low heat, stirring occasionally, for 5 minutes, until softened. Add the tomato paste, water, tomatoes, and bring to a boil. Reduce the heat and simmer for 15–20 minutes.

4 Remove the pan from the oven and let cool for 10 minutes. Drain off any excess liquid and invert onto a board. Cut into slices and serve with the tomato sauce.

classic lasagna

ingredients

serves 4

2 tablespoons olive oil
2 ounces pancetta or bacon, chopped
1 garlic clove, finely chopped
1 onion, chopped
8 ounces ground round beef
2 carrots, chopped
2 celery stalks, chopped
2 cups chopped white button mushrooms
pinch of dried oregano
1/3 cup red wine
2/3 cup beef stock
1 tablespoon tomato paste
8 ounces dried oven-ready lasagna noodles
1 cup grated Parmesan cheese
1 (14 1/2-ounce) can diced tomatoes
few fresh basil leaves, torn
salt and pepper
mixed salad, to serve

method

1 Heat the oil in a large saucepan. Add the pancetta and cook over medium heat, stirring occasionally, for 2–3 minutes. Reduce the heat to low, add the garlic and onion, and cook, stirring occasionally, for 5 minutes, until softened.

2 Add the beef, increase the heat to medium, and cook, stirring frequently and breaking it up with a wooden spoon, for 8–10 minutes, until evenly browned. Stir in the carrots, celery, and mushrooms and cook, stirring occasionally, for an additional 5 minutes. Add the oregano, pour in the wine and stock, and stir in the tomato paste. Season with salt and pepper. Bring to a boil, reduce the heat, and simmer for 40 minutes.

3 Preheat the oven to 375°F. Make alternating layers of the beef sauce, lasagna noodles, and Parmesan in a large, rectangular ovenproof dish. Pour the tomatoes over the top to cover completely. Bake in the preheated oven for 30 minutes. Remove the dish from the oven and let stand for 10 minutes, then sprinkle with torn basil, divide among four plates, and serve with a mixed salad.

chicken lasagna

ingredients

serves 6

2 tablespoons olive oil
2 pounds ground chicken
1 garlic clove, finely chopped
4 carrots, chopped
4 leeks, sliced
2 cups chicken stock
2 tablespoons tomato paste
1 cup shredded cheddar cheese
1 teaspoon Dijon mustard
4 ounces dried oven-ready
    lasagna noodles
salt and pepper

white sauce

2½ cups milk
4 tablespoons butter
½ cup all-purpose flour

method

1 Preheat the oven to 375°F. Heat the oil in a heavy saucepan. Add the chicken and cook over medium heat, breaking it up with a wooden spoon, for 5 minutes, or until it is browned all over. Add the garlic, carrots, and leeks and cook, stirring occasionally, for 5 minutes.

2 Stir in the stock and tomato paste and season with salt and pepper. Bring to a boil, reduce the heat, cover, and simmer for 30 minutes.

3 Meanwhile, make the white sauce. Heat the milk, butter, and flour in a saucepan, beating continuously, until smooth and thick. Season with salt and pepper, and stir in half the cheese and the mustard.

4 In a large ovenproof dish, make alternate layers of the chicken mixture, lasagna noodles, and cheese sauce, ending with a layer of cheese sauce. Sprinkle with the remaining cheese and bake in the preheated oven for 1 hour, or until golden brown and bubbling. Serve the lasagna immediately.

chicken & mushroom lasagna

ingredients

serves 4–6

2 tablespoons olive oil
1 large onion, finely chopped
1 pound ground chicken or
    ground turkey
4 ounces pancetta, chopped
4 cups chopped cremini
    mushrooms
4 ounces dried porcini, soaked
$\frac{2}{3}$ cup dry white wine
1 (14$\frac{1}{2}$-ounce) can diced tomatoes
3 tablespoons chopped fresh basil
9 dried oven-ready
    lasagna noodles
3 tablespoons finely grated
    Parmesan cheese
salt and pepper

white sauce

2$\frac{1}{2}$ cups milk
4 tablespoons butter
$\frac{1}{2}$ cup all-purpose flour

method

1 Preheat the oven to 375°F. For the white sauce, heat the milk, butter, and flour in a saucepan, beating continuously, until smooth and thick. Season with salt and pepper, cover, and let stand.

2 Heat the oil in a large saucepan and sauté the onion, stirring, for 3–4 minutes. Add the chicken and pancetta and cook for 6–8 minutes. Stir in both types of mushrooms and cook for an additional 2–3 minutes.

3 Add the wine and bring to a boil. Pour in the tomatoes and their can juices, cover, reduce the heat, and simmer for 20 minutes. Stir in the basil.

4 Arrange three of the lasagna noodles in a rectangular ovenproof dish, then spoon over one-third of the meat sauce. Spread one-third of the white sauce over the meat. Repeat the layers twice, finishing with a layer of white sauce.

5 Sprinkle with the cheese and bake in the preheated oven for 35–40 minutes, until the topping is golden and bubbling. Serve immediately.

turkey noodle casserole

ingredients

serves 4–6

1 stick butter
1 tablespoon olive oil
1 onion, finely chopped
1 pound ground turkey
2 tablespoons all-purpose flour
3 cups milk
1 teaspoon Dijon mustard
¾ cup shredded American cheese
   or cheddar cheese
10 ounces dried macaroni
2 tablespoons chopped fresh
   parsley
2 cups fresh bread crumbs
salt

method

1 Melt 2 tablespoons of the butter with the oil in a skillet. Add the onion and cook over low heat, stirring occasionally, for 5 minutes until soft. Add the turkey, increase the heat to medium and cook, stirring frequently, for 7–8 minutes, until evenly browned. Remove the skillet from the heat, transfer the turkey and onion to a bowl with a slotted spoon, and set aside.

2 Melt 3 tablespoons of the remaining butter in a saucepan. Stir in the flour and cook, stirring continuously, for 1 minute. Remove the pan from the heat and gradually beat in the milk, then return to the heat and bring to a boil, beating continuously until thickened. Remove the pan from the heat and stir in the mustard, turkey mixture, and ½ cup of the cheese.

3 Preheat the oven to 350°F. Bring a large saucepan of lightly salted water to a boil. Add the pasta, return to a boil, and cook according to the package directions, until tender but still firm to the bite. Drain and stir into the turkey mixture with the parsley.

4 Spoon the mixture into an ovenproof dish, sprinkle with the bread crumbs and remaining cheese, and dab with the remaining butter. Bake in the preheated oven for 25 minutes, until golden and bubbling. Serve immediately.

beef & macaroni soufflé

ingredients

serves 4

2 tablespoons olive oil
1 large onion, chopped
8 ounces ground round beef
1 garlic clove, finely chopped
1 (14½-ounce) can diced tomatoes
1 tablespoon tomato paste
6 ounces dried macaroni
butter, for greasing
3 eggs, separated
½ cup freshly grated Parmesan
    cheese, plus extra to serve
salt and pepper

method

1 Preheat the oven to 375°F. Heat the oil in a large, heavy skillet. Add the onion and cook over low heat, stirring occasionally, for 5 minutes, or until softened. Add the beef and cook, breaking up the meat with a wooden spoon, until browned. Stir in the garlic, tomatoes and their can juices, and tomato paste, then season with salt and pepper. Bring to a boil, reduce the heat, and simmer for 20 minutes, then remove the skillet from the heat and let cool slightly.

2 Meanwhile, bring a large, heavy saucepan of lightly salted water to a boil. Add the pasta, return to a boil, and cook according to the package directions, until tender but still firm to the bite. Drain and reserve.

3 Lightly grease a 1½-quart soufflé dish with butter. Beat the egg yolks and add them to the meat sauce, then stir in the pasta. Whisk the egg whites until stiff peaks form, then fold into the pasta mixture. Spoon the mixture into the dish, sprinkle with the grated Parmesan cheese, and bake in the preheated oven for 45 minutes, or until well risen and golden brown. Sprinkle with extra grated Parmesan cheese and serve immediately.

greek pasta casserole

ingredients

serves 4

1 tablespoon olive oil
1 onion, chopped
2 garlic cloves, finely chopped
1 pound ground round beef
2 tablespoons tomato paste
2 tablespoons all-purpose flour
1¼ cups chicken stock
1 teaspoon ground cinnamon
4 ounces dried macaroni
2 beefsteak tomatoes, sliced
1¼ cups Greek-style yogurt
2 eggs, lightly beaten
salt and pepper

method

1 Preheat the oven to 375°F. Heat the oil in a large, heavy skillet. Add the onion and garlic and cook over low heat, stirring occasionally, for 5 minutes, or until softened. Add the ground beef and cook, breaking it up with a wooden spoon, until browned all over. Add the tomato paste and sprinkle in the flour. Cook, stirring, for 1 minute, then stir in the stock. Season with salt and pepper and stir in the cinnamon. Bring to a boil, reduce the heat, cover, and cook for 25 minutes.

2 Meanwhile, bring a large saucepan of lightly salted water to a boil. Add the pasta, return to a boil, and cook according to the package directions, until tender but still firm to the bite.

3 Drain the pasta and stir into the beef mixture. Spoon into a large ovenproof dish and arrange the tomato slices on top. Beat together the yogurt and eggs, then spoon evenly over the beef mixture. Bake the dish in the preheated oven for 1 hour, until golden and bubbling. Serve immediately.

layered beef & feta casserole

ingredients

serves 6

1/4 cup olive oil
1 onion, chopped
2 garlic cloves, finely chopped
1 1/2 pounds ground round beef
1 1/2 tablespoons tomato paste
1 (28-ounce) can diced tomatoes
2 tablespoons Worcestershire sauce
1 tablespoon chopped fresh
    oregano
6 russet potatoes
2 eggplants, sliced
1 cup feta cheese
2 1/2 cups Greek-style yogurt
3 extra-large eggs, lightly beaten
1/2 cup grated Parmesan cheese
salt and pepper

method

1 Heat half the oil in a large skillet. Add the onion and garlic and cook over low heat for 5 minutes, until softened. Add the beef, increase the heat to medium, and cook, stirring frequently and breaking up the meat with a wooden spoon, for 8–10 minutes, until evenly browned. Drain off the fat. Stir in the tomato paste and cook for an additional 2–3 minutes, then stir in the tomatoes, Worcestershire sauce, and oregano. Season with salt and pepper. Reduce the heat, cover, and simmer for 30 minutes. Meanwhile, cook the potatoes in a saucepan of salted boiling water for 15 minutes. Drain and let cool slightly, then cut into thick slices.

2 Preheat the oven to 350°F. Brush the eggplant slices with the remaining oil. Heat a large, heavy skillet. Add the eggplant slices, in batches, and cook over medium heat for 3 minutes on each side, until softened. Drain on paper towels.

3 Transfer the beef mixture to an ovenproof dish and cover with the potato slices, followed by the eggplant slices. Crumble the feta over the top. Mix the yogurt, eggs, and half the Parmesan in a bowl and pour over the dish. Sprinkle with the remaining Parmesan and bake in the preheated oven for 30–35 minutes, until golden brown. Serve immediately.

moussaka

ingredients

serves 4

2 eggplants, thinly sliced
1 pound ground round beef or
    ground lamb
2 onions, thinly sliced
1 teaspoon finely chopped garlic
1 (14½-ounce) can diced tomatoes
2 tablespoons chopped
    fresh parsley
2 eggs
1¼ cups Greek-style yogurt
1 tablespoon freshly grated
    Parmesan cheese
salt and pepper

method

1 Dry-fry the eggplant slices, in batches, in a nonstick skillet on both sides until brown. Remove from the skillet.

2 Add the beef to the skillet and cook for 5 minutes, stirring, until evenly browned. Stir in the onions and garlic and cook for an additional 5 minutes, or until brown. Add the tomatoes, parsley, and salt and pepper, then bring to a boil, reduce the heat, and simmer for 20 minutes, or until the meat is tender.

3 Preheat the oven to 350°F. Arrange one-third of the eggplant slices in a layer in an ovenproof dish. Add half the meat mixture, then half the remaining eggplant slices. Add the remaining meat mixture and layer the remaining eggplant slices on top.

4 Beat the eggs in a bowl, then beat in the yogurt and season with salt and pepper. Pour the mixture over the eggplants and sprinkle the grated cheese on top.

5 Bake the moussaka in the preheated oven for 45 minutes, or until golden brown. Serve straight from the dish.

beef & mashed potato casserole

ingredients

serves 6

6 russet potatoes, cut into chunks
1 cup shredded American or
    cheddar cheese
2 tablespoons sunflower oil
1 onion, chopped
1 garlic clove, chopped
2 carrots, chopped
1 pound ground round beef
2 cups sliced white button
    mushrooms
1¼ cups hot beef stock
1 teaspoon sugar
1 tablespoon Worcestershire sauce
salt and pepper

method

1 Cook the potatoes in a large saucepan of salted boiling water for 20–25 minutes, until tender but not falling apart. Drain the potatoes, return to the pan, and mash well, then stir in three-quarters of the cheese.

2 Meanwhile, heat the oil in a saucepan. Add the onion, garlic, and carrots and cook over low heat, stirring occasionally, for 5 minutes, until softened. Increase the heat to medium, add the beef, and cook, stirring frequently and breaking it up with a wooden spoon, for 8–10 minutes, until evenly browned.

3 Add the mushrooms and cook for 2 minutes, then pour in the stock and stir in the sugar and Worcestershire sauce. Season with salt and pepper. Reduce the heat, cover, and simmer for 20 minutes.

4 Preheat the oven to 400°F. Spoon the meat mixture into an ovenproof dish and spread the potato over the top. Sprinkle with the remaining cheese and bake in the preheated oven for 20 minutes, until the topping is golden brown. Serve immediately.

variation

Use 1 pound ground lamb instead of beef, omit the mushrooms, and substitute 2 tablespoons of tomato paste for the sugar.

beef 'n' beans

ingredients

serves 4

1 onion, chopped
1 pound ground round beef
1 (15-ounce) can baked beans
1 tablespoon maple syrup
1 tablespoon mild mustard
1 tablespoon concentrated
    beef stock
6 russet potatoes, diced
½ cup cream cheese
salt and pepper

method

1 Put the onion and beef into a large nonstick skillet and cook over medium heat, stirring frequently and breaking up the meat with a wooden spoon, for 8–10 minutes, until evenly browned.

2 Stir the baked beans, maple syrup, mustard, and concentrated stock into the skillet and season with pepper. Reduce the heat, cover, and simmer, stirring occasionally and adding a little water if the mixture seems to be drying out, for 15 minutes.

3 Meanwhile, preheat the broiler. Cook the potatoes in a saucepan of salted boiling water for 20 minutes, until tender but not falling apart. Drain the potatoes and return to the pan. Add the cream cheese, season with salt and pepper, and mash until smooth.

4 Transfer the beef mixture to an ovenproof dish and spread the mashed potato over the top. Cook under the preheated broiler for 5 minutes, until the topping is golden brown. Serve immediately.

beef with garlic potatoes

ingredients

serves 4

4 russet potatoes
3 tablespoons olive oil
1 onion, chopped
1 pound ground round beef
4 carrots, chopped
4 tomatoes, peeled and chopped
1 teaspoon cornstarch
1¼ cups hot beef stock
1 tablespoon chopped
    fresh parsley
1 teaspoon chopped fresh sage
3 garlic cloves, finely chopped
salt and pepper

method

1 Preheat the oven to 350°F. Parboil the potatoes in a saucepan of salted boiling water for 15 minutes, then drain and let cool.

2 Meanwhile, heat 1 tablespoon of the oil in a large saucepan. Add the onion and cook over low heat, stirring occasionally, for 5 minutes, until softened.

3 Add the beef, increase the heat to medium, and cook, stirring frequently and breaking it up with a wooden spoon, for 8–10 minutes, until evenly browned. Add the carrots and tomatoes. Stir the cornstarch into the stock, then stir the mixture into the pan. Season with salt and pepper. Stir in the parsley and sage and bring to a boil, then reduce the heat and simmer for 5 minutes.

4 Meanwhile, cut the potatoes into slices. Mix together the garlic and the remaining oil in a small bowl and season with salt and pepper.

5 Transfer the beef mixture to an ovenproof dish and arrange the potato slices on top. Brush the garlic-flavored oil over them and bake in the preheated oven for 30–35 minutes, until the topping is golden brown. Serve immediately.

baked beef & potato layers

ingredients

serves 4

3½ tablespoons tomato paste
½ cup water
1 (14½-ounce) can diced tomatoes
1 tablespoon chopped fresh thyme
4 russet potatoes
3 tablespoons butter, plus extra
    for greasing
8 fresh ground round beef
1 egg, lightly beaten
2 onions, sliced
1 cup shredded American cheese
    or cheddar cheese
salt and pepper

method

1 Heat the tomato paste, water, tomatoes, and thyme in a saucepan. Season with salt and pepper. Bring to a boil, then reduce the heat and simmer, stirring occasionally, for 30 minutes, until thickened. Meanwhile, cook the potatoes in a saucepan of salted boiling water for 15 minutes. Drain and let cool slightly, then cut into ¼-inch slices.

2 Preheat the oven to 350°F. Grease an ovenproof dish with butter.

3 Mix together the beef and egg in a bowl and season with salt and pepper. Divide the mixture into six portions and shape each into a patty about ¼ inch thick. Melt 2 tablespoons of the butter in a skillet. Add the patties and cook over medium heat for 3 minutes on each side, until lightly browned. Remove with a spatula. Add the onions to the skillet and cook over low heat for 5 minutes, until softened.

4 Put half the potato slices in the bottom of the prepared dish. Cover with the beef patties, followed by the onions, then sprinkle with half the cheese. Top with the remaining potato slices and pour the tomato mixture over the top. Sprinkle with the remaining cheese, dab with the remaining butter, and bake in the preheated oven for 20 minutes. Serve immediately.

beef & cheese with biscuit topping

ingredients

serves 4

2 tablespoons sunflower oil
1 pound ground round beef
2 tablespoons all-purpose flour
4 onions, cut into wedges
2 tablespoons ketchup
1 tablespoon chopped fresh thyme
1 bay leaf
1¼ cups beef stock
salt and pepper

biscuit topping

1¾ cups all-purpose flour,
    plus extra for dusting
2¾ teaspoons baking powder
½ teaspoon dry mustard
pinch of salt
3 tablespoons butter, cut into
    small pieces
¾ cup shredded American cheese
    or cheddar cheese
dash of Tabasco sauce
milk, for glazing

method

1 Preheat the oven to 350°F. Heat the oil in a skillet. Add the beef and cook over medium heat, stirring frequently and breaking it up with a wooden spoon, for 8–10 minutes, until the beef is evenly browned.

2 Spoon the beef into a casserole dish, then stir in the all-purpose flour. Add the onions, ketchup, thyme, and bay leaf and season with salt and pepper. Pour in the stock and stir well, then cover and bake in the preheated oven for 1 hour.

3 Meanwhile, to make the topping, sift the flour, baking powder, mustard, and salt into a bowl. Add the butter and rub it in with your fingertips until the mixture resembles bread crumbs. Stir in the cheese, Tabasco sauce, and enough water to mix to a soft dough.

4 Roll out the dough to a thickness of ½ inch on a lightly floured surface, then stamp out circles with a 2½-inch fluted round cutter.

5 Remove the casserole from the oven and take off the lid. Remove and discard the bay leaf. Cover the beef mixture with the dough circles and brush them with milk. Return the casserole dish, without the lid, to the oven and bake for an additional 35 minutes, until the topping is golden brown. Serve immediately.

beef & vegetable casserole

ingredients

serves 6–8

3 tablespoons sunflower oil
2 garlic cloves, finely chopped
2 onions, sliced
2¼ pounds ground round beef
3 zucchini, thinly sliced
5 carrots, thinly sliced
1 red bell pepper, seeded and
    thinly sliced
⅓ cup raisins
6 tablespoons butter
⅔ cup all-purpose flour
3½ cups milk
1 cup shredded Monterey Jack
    cheese or cheddar cheese,
1 (11-ounce) can corn kernels,
    drained
1 (15-ounce) can cannellini
    beans, drained and rinsed
2 tablespoons chopped fresh
    parsley
4 egg yolks
salt and pepper

method

1 Heat the oil in a large saucepan. Add the garlic and onions and cook over low heat, stirring occasionally, for 5 minutes, until softened. Add the beef, increase the heat to medium, and cook, stirring frequently and breaking it up with a wooden spoon, for 8–10 minutes, until evenly browned. Stir in the zucchini, carrots, red bell pepper, and raisins and season with salt and pepper. Reduce the heat, cover, and simmer for 25 minutes.

2 Meanwhile, preheat the oven to 350°F. Melt the butter in a saucepan. Add the flour and cook over low heat, stirring continuously, for 2 minutes. Gradually stir in the milk, a little at a time, until smooth and thickened. Remove the pan from the heat and stir in the cheese until melted.

3 Stir the corn, beans, and parsley into the beef mixture and simmer for an additional 3 minutes, then remove the pan from the heat. Spoon the mixture into an ovenproof dish.

4 Lightly beat the egg yolks in a bowl with a fork, then stir in ¼ cup of the cheese sauce. Stir the egg yolk mixture into the cheese sauce and pour it over the meat mixture to cover. Bake in the preheated oven for 25–30 minutes, until the topping is golden brown. Serve immediately.

upside-down pie

ingredients

serves 4

3 tablespoons sunflower oil
2 onions, finely chopped
1 garlic clove, finely chopped
12 ounces ground round beef
1 cup finely chopped white button
   mushrooms
4 tomatoes, peeled and diced
½ teaspoon anchovy paste
1 tablespoon Worcestershire sauce
1 teaspoon dried oregano
1 bay leaf
⅔ cup beef stock
⅔ cup red wine
salt and pepper

crust dough

1⅓ cups all-purpose flour
2 teaspoons baking powder
pinch of salt
4 tablespoons butter, cut into
   small pieces
¾ cup shredded cheddar cheese
1 egg yolk
½–⅓ cup milk

method

1 Heat the oil in a saucepan. Add the onions and garlic
and cook over low heat, stirring occasionally, for
5 minutes, until softened. Add the beef, increase the
heat to medium, and cook, stirring frequently and
breaking it up with a wooden spoon, for 8–10 minutes,
until evenly browned.

2 Add the mushrooms and tomatoes and cook for an
additional 3 minutes, then stir in the anchovy paste,
Worcestershire sauce, oregano, bay leaf, stock, and
wine. Season with salt and pepper. Bring to a boil,
then reduce the heat and simmer, stirring occasionally,
for 20 minutes.

3 Meanwhile, preheat the oven to 350°F. Sift the flour,
baking powder, and salt into a bowl. Add the butter
and rub it in with your fingertips until the mixture
resembles bread crumbs. Stir in the cheese, then add
the egg yolk and enough of the milk to mix to a soft
dough. Shape the dough into an 8-inch circle.

4 Transfer the beef mixture to an 8-inch round cake pan
and put the dough circle on top. Bake in the preheated
oven for 50 minutes, until the topping is golden brown.
Remove the pan from the oven and invert onto a warm
serving dish. Cut into wedges and serve immediately.

ground beef casserole

ingredients

serves 6

⅓ cup olive oil, plus extra if needed
2¼ pounds ground round beef
6 scallions, chopped
6 tomatoes, peeled and chopped
1 red bell pepper, seeded
    and sliced
2 slices fresh pineapple
    (about ¾ inch thick), peeled,
    cored, and chopped,
    or 2 slices canned pineapple,
    drained and chopped
1 tablespoon chopped fresh thyme
2 eggplants, thinly sliced
1½ cups shredded cheddar cheese
salt and pepper

method

1 Heat 2 tablespoons of the oil in a large skillet. Add the beef and cook over medium heat, stirring frequently and breaking it up with a wooden spoon, for 8–10 minutes, until lightly browned. Stir in the scallions, tomatoes, red bell pepper, and pineapple and cook, stirring occasionally, for an additional 5 minutes. Stir in the thyme and season with salt and pepper. Reduce the heat and simmer, stirring occasionally, for 15 minutes.

2 Preheat the oven to 350°F. Heat the remaining oil in a skillet. Add the eggplant slices, in batches, and cook for 2–3 minutes on each side, until softened. Add more oil to the skillet as required. Remove the eggplant slices from the skillet and drain them on paper towels.

3 Put one-third of the eggplant slices in an ovenproof dish and add half the beef mixture. Add half the remaining eggplant slices and top with the remaining beef mixture. Cover with the remaining eggplant slices, sprinkle with the cheese, and bake in the preheated oven for 30 minutes, until the topping is golden brown. Serve immediately.

beef goulash

ingredients

serves 6

1 tablespoon olive oil
1 pound ground round beef
2 onions, finely chopped
2 garlic cloves, finely chopped
2 tablespoons all-purpose flour
1 cup water
1 (14¹/₂-ounce) can diced tomatoes
1 carrot, finely chopped
2 red bell peppers, roasted, peeled,
    seeded, and chopped
1 teaspoon Hungarian paprika
¹/₄ teaspoon caraway seeds
pinch of dried oregano
4 cups beef stock
2 ounces dried tagliatelle,
    broken into small pieces
salt and pepper
sour cream and fresh cilantro
    sprigs, to garnish

method

1 Preheat the oven to 325°F. Heat the oil in a large, flameproof casserole dish over medium–high heat. Add the beef and sprinkle with salt and pepper. Cook until lightly browned.

2 Reduce the heat and add the onions and garlic. Cook for about 3 minutes, stirring frequently, until the onions are softened. Stir in the flour and continue cooking for 1 minute.

3 Add the water and stir to combine well, scraping the bottom of the dish to mix in the flour. Stir in the tomatoes, carrot, red bell peppers, paprika, caraway seeds, oregano, and stock.

4 Cover and cook in the preheated oven for 1 hour, until all the vegetables are tender.

5 Meanwhile, bring a large saucepan of salted water to a boil. Add the pasta, return to a boil, and cook according to the package directions, until tender but still firm to the bite. Drain and stir into the goulash.

6 Taste and adjust the seasoning, if necessary. Ladle into warm bowls and top each with a tablespoonful of sour cream. Garnish with cilantro and serve.

something spicy

turkey & chorizo empanadas

ingredients

serves 8

2 tablespoons vegetable oil,
    plus extra for greasing
1 onion, finely chopped
2 garlic cloves, finely chopped
8 ounces ground turkey
2 ounces chorizo sausage,
    finely chopped
2 teaspoons smoked paprika
1 yellow bell pepper, seeded
    and finely chopped
½ cup frozen peas
2 tablespoons fresh flat-leaf
    parsley, finely chopped
all-purpose flour, for dusting
1 (15-ounce) package rolled
    dough pie crusts
1 small egg, beaten
salt and pepper

method

1 Preheat the oven to 350°F. Lightly grease a baking sheet with oil. Heat the oil in a nonstick skillet, add the onion, and cook for 4–5 minutes, until softened. Add the garlic and cook for an additional 1 minute.

2 Add the ground turkey, chorizo, paprika, and yellow bell pepper and continue to cook for an additional 6–8 minutes, until the turkey is evenly browned. Stir in the peas, and parsley and season with salt and pepper.

3 Roll out the dough pie crusts on a lightly floured surface and use a saucer to cut out eight circles. Spoon a small amount of the filling onto one half of each circle. Use a pastry brush to brush the edges of the dough with a little beaten egg and fold the circles in half over the filling, crimping together the edges to form a tight seal.

4 Place the empanadas on the prepared baking sheet and brush each one with the remaining beaten egg. Bake in the preheated oven for 15–18 minutes, until golden. Serve immediately.

quesadillas

ingredients

serves 4

1 pound ground round beef
1 onion, finely chopped
1 red bell pepper, seeded and
  finely chopped
1 garlic clove, crushed
1 teaspoon smoked paprika
$\frac{1}{2}$ teaspoon cumin seeds
$\frac{1}{2}$ fresh red chile, seeded and
  finely chopped
$\frac{1}{4}$ cup tomato paste
1 (15-ounce) can red kidney
  beans, drained and rinsed
vegetable oil spray
8 flour tortillas
$\frac{3}{4}$ cup shredded Monterey Jack
  cheese or cheddar cheese
salt and pepper
tomato salsa, to serve

method

1 Dry-fry the ground beef in a nonstick skillet for 4–5 minutes, until starting to brown.

2 Add the onion, red bell pepper, and garlic and cook for an additional 1–2 minutes. Add the paprika, cumin seeds, and chile and cook for 1 minute. Add the tomato paste and beans, then season with salt and pepper. Cover and cook for 10 minutes, until the meat is thoroughly cooked.

3 Preheat the oven to 275°F. Heat a nonstick skillet over medium heat and spray with the oil. Place a tortilla in the pan and spoon about one-quarter of the meat mixture over it, spreading the sauce across the surface of the tortilla. Sprinkle with some cheese, top with another tortilla, and press down. Cook in the skillet for 1–2 minutes, then invert onto a plate and slide back into the skillet to cook the other side for an additional 1–2 minutes. Transfer to a baking sheet, cover, and place in the preheated oven to keep warm while cooking the remaining tortillas.

4 Serve the warm quesadillas cut into quarters with some tomato salsa.

beef enchiladas

ingredients

serves 4

1 pound ground round beef
1 onion, finely chopped
2 garlic cloves, finely chopped
1 tablespoon cumin seeds
1 teaspoon ground cinnamon
2 teaspoons hot chili powder
1 teaspoon ground coriander
2 tablespoons tomato paste
1 (14½-ounce) can diced tomatoes
½ cup red wine
½ cup water
8 small flour tortillas
½ cup shredded Monterey Jack
   cheese or cheddar cheese
salt and pepper

method

1 Dry-fry the ground beef in a nonstick skillet for 4–5 minutes, until starting to brown. Add the onion and garlic and cook for an additional 1–2 minutes.

2 Add the cumin seeds, cinnamon, chili powder, and coriander and cook, stirring continuously, for 1–2 minutes, until the spices are lightly toasted. Stir in the tomato paste and cook for an additional minute.

3 Add half the tomatoes, the red wine, and water, then season with salt and pepper. Stir well, cover, and simmer for about 10 minutes, until the beef is thoroughly cooked.

4 Preheat the oven to 350°F. Spoon some of the chili filling in a line down the center of each tortilla and fold in the ends and sides to form a package.

5 Place the enchiladas, seam side down, in an ovenproof dish and spoon over the remaining diced tomatoes. Sprinkle with the cheese and bake in the preheated oven for 10 minutes, until the cheese is just golden. Serve immediately.

beef burritos

ingredients

serves 4

1 pound ground round beef
1 onion, finely chopped
1 yellow bell pepper, seeded
   and finely chopped
1 garlic clove, crushed
½ teaspoon cumin seeds
1 teaspoon dried oregano
1 fresh red chile, seeded and
   finely chopped
¼ cup tomato paste
1 (15-ounce) can red kidney
   beans, drained and rinsed
8 large flour tortillas
vegetable oil spray
¼ cup shredded cheddar cheese
salt and pepper
tomato salsa, to serve

method

1 Dry-fry the ground beef in a nonstick skillet for 4–5 minutes, until starting to brown.

2 Add the onion, yellow bell pepper, and garlic and cook for an additional 1–2 minutes. Add the cumin seeds, oregano, chile, tomato paste, and beans, and season with salt and pepper. Cover and cook for 10 minutes, until the meat is thoroughly cooked.

3 Warm the tortillas in a skillet, sprayed with oil, over medium heat. Fill the tortillas with the ground beef mixture, sprinkle with the cheese, wrap to form a package, and serve with tomato salsa.

beef tacos

ingredients

serves 4

1 pound ground round beef
1 onion, finely chopped
1 yellow bell pepper, seeded and
    finely chopped
1 garlic clove crushed
1 teaspoon smoked paprika
½ teaspoon cumin seeds
1 fresh red chile, seeded and finely
    chopped
¼ cup tomato paste
¾ cup drained, canned
    kidney beans
salt and pepper

to serve

taco shells
shredded iceberg lettuce
grated Monterey Jack cheese,
    American cheese, or
    cheddar cheese
sour cream
chopped avocado

method

1 Dry-fry the ground beef in a nonstick skillet for
    4–5 minutes, until lightly browned.

2 Add the onion, yellow bell pepper, and garlic and cook
    for an additional 1–2 minutes. Add the paprika,
    cumin seeds, and chile, and cook for 1 minute.
    Add the tomato paste and kidney beans, then season
    with salt and pepper, cover, and cook for 10 minutes,
    until the meat is thoroughly cooked.

3 Warm the taco shells according to the package
    directions. Spoon the spicy meat mixture into the
    shells and serve topped with lettuce, cheese, sour
    cream, and avocado.

variation

Use 1 pound ground chicken instead of beef. Omit the
smoked paprika and cumin. After adding the salt and
pepper, add 1 (14½-ounce) can diced tomatoes. Bring to
a boil. Reduce the heat to medium–low, cover, and cook
for 10 minutes. Serve in taco shells.

beef with pimientos

ingredients

serves 4

2 tablespoons olive oil

3 large onions, thinly sliced
into rings

2 garlic cloves, finely chopped

1½ pounds ground round beef

2 tablespoons Worcestershire sauce

3 tablespoons lemon juice

1 teaspoon hot paprika

1 tablespoon packed light
brown sugar

2 pimientos from a can or jar,
drained and sliced lengthwise

salt and pepper

method

1 Heat the oil in a large skillet. Add the onions and garlic and cook over low heat, stirring occasionally, for 5 minutes, until softened. Add the beef, increase the heat to medium, and cook, stirring frequently and breaking up the meat with a wooden spoon, for 8–10 minutes, until evenly browned.

2 Stir in the Worcestershire sauce, lemon juice, paprika, and sugar. Season with salt and pepper, then cook, stirring frequently, for 5 minutes. Add the pimientos, reduce the heat, and simmer, stirring occasionally, for 20 minutes, until the meat is cooked through and tender. Serve immediately.

stir-fried beef

ingredients

serves 6

⅓ cup Chinese rice wine or
    dry sherry
3 garlic cloves, finely chopped
2 tablespoons finely chopped
    fresh ginger
1 tablespoon dark soy sauce
1 teaspoon sesame oil
1 tablespoon cornstarch
2 pounds ground sirloin beef
3 tablespoons peanut oil
2 tablespoons hoisin sauce
2 tablespoons oyster sauce
2 teaspoons rice vinegar
2 carrots, thinly sliced diagonally
4 scallions, thinly sliced lengthwise
3 cups broccoli florets
1 large red bell pepper, seeded
    and thinly sliced
12 baby corn

method

1 Mix together half the rice wine, the garlic, ginger, soy sauce, sesame oil, and cornstarch in a bowl. Add the beef, turning and stirring to coat, cover with plastic wrap, and let marinate in the refrigerator for 1 hour.

2 Heat a wok or large skillet over medium heat, then add the peanut oil, swirl it around the wok, and heat. Remove the beef from the bowl, add it to the wok, and stir-fry, breaking it up with a wooden spoon, for 3–5 minutes, until evenly browned.

3 Stir in the remaining rice wine, the hoisin sauce, oyster sauce, and vinegar and cook, stirring continuously, for 1 minute.

4 Stir in the carrots, scallions, broccoli, red bell pepper, and baby corn and stir-fry for an additional 3–4 minutes, until the vegetables are just tender. Serve immediately.

beef soup with ginger & lemongrass

ingredients

serves 6

½ ounce dried cellophane noodles
8 ounces ground sirloin beef
2 shallots, finely chopped
¼ cup Thai fish sauce
2 tablespoons peanut oil
½ cup long-grain rice
1 teaspoon grated fresh ginger
6½ cups water
1 tablespoon packed brown sugar
2 garlic cloves, finely chopped
1 tablespoon finely chopped
    lemongrass
2 tablespoons crushed unsalted
    roasted peanuts
2 scallions, thinly sliced
1 tablespoon chopped fresh
    cilantro
salt and pepper

method

1 Prepare the noodles according to the package directions, until soft. Drain and cut into 2-inch lengths.

2 Put the beef, shallots, and 1 tablespoon of the fish sauce into a large bowl, season with pepper, and mix well. Cover with plastic wrap and chill in the refrigerator until required.

3 Heat half the oil in a large saucepan. Add the rice and ginger and cook over low heat, stirring continuously, for 1 minute. Pour in the water, increase the heat to medium, and bring to a boil. Partly cover the pan, reduce the heat, and simmer for 20 minutes, until the rice is tender. Stir in the sugar and the remaining fish sauce and season with salt.

4 Heat the remaining oil in a small skillet. Add the garlic and lemongrass and cook over low–medium heat, stirring continuously, for 1 minute, then stir into the rice mixture with the noodles and the beef mixture. Bring back to a boil, stirring continuously and breaking up the meat with a wooden spoon. Pour into warm soup bowls and sprinkle with the peanuts, scallions, and cilantro. Serve immediately.

sichuan beef & noodles

ingredients

serves 4

8 ounces thick rice noodles
1 tablespoon cornstarch
3 tablespoons soy sauce
1½ tablespoons Chinese rice wine
1½ teaspoons sugar
1½ teaspoons sesame oil
12 ounces ground sirloin beef
1½ tablespoons peanut oil
2 large garlic cloves,
    finely chopped
1 large fresh red chile, or to taste,
    seeded and thinly sliced
3 scallions, finely chopped
finely chopped fresh cilantro,
    to garnish

method

1 Prepare the noodles according to the package directions, until tender. Drain well and set aside.

2 Meanwhile, put the cornstarch in a separate bowl, and add the soy sauce, rice wine, sugar, and sesame oil, stirring until smooth. Add the ground beef and use your hands to toss together the ingredients without squeezing the beef. Set aside to marinate for 10 minutes.

3 Heat a wok or skillet over high heat, then add the peanut oil. Add the garlic, chile, and scallions and stir-fry for about 30 seconds. Add the ground beef along with any marinade left in the bowl and stir-fry for an additional 5 minutes, or until the beef is no longer pink. Add the noodles and use two forks to mix together. Sprinkle with the chopped cilantro and serve.

beef with red pepper, fruit & nuts

ingredients

serves 4

3 tablespoons sunflower oil
2 onions, finely chopped
2 garlic cloves, finely chopped
2 celery stalks, chopped
1 red bell pepper, seeded
    and chopped
2¼ pounds ground sirloin beef
1 (14½-ounce) can diced tomatoes
1 (15-ounce) can navy beans,
    drained and rinsed
⅓ cup tomato paste
1 teaspoon chili powder
½ teaspoon ground nutmeg
2 Granny Smith apples, cored
    and chopped
½ cup chopped dried apricots
2 tablespoons slivered almonds,
    plus extra to garnish
1 cup frozen green beans, thawed
salt and pepper

method

1 Heat the oil in a large skillet. Add the onions, garlic, celery, and red bell pepper and cook over low heat, stirring occasionally, for 5 minutes, until softened. Add the beef, increase the heat to medium, and cook, stirring frequently and breaking it up with a wooden spoon, for 8–10 minutes, until evenly browned.

2 Add the tomatoes, navy beans, tomato paste, chili powder, nutmeg, apples, apricots, almonds, and green beans. Season with salt and pepper. Reduce the heat, cover, and simmer for 30 minutes, then remove the lid and simmer for an additional 10 minutes.

3 Serve immediately, garnished with slivered almonds.

thai chicken cakes

ingredients

serves 4

½ bunch scallions, trimmed and
   coarsely chopped
1¼-inch piece fresh ginger,
   coarsely chopped
3 garlic cloves, crushed
handful fresh cilantro, including
   the stems
1 red chile, seeded and
   coarsely chopped
1 pound ground chicken
2 tablespoons light soy sauce
dash Thai fish sauce
1 egg white
2 tablespoons all-purpose flour
finely grated zest of 1 lime
2–3 tablespoons vegetable oil,
   for frying
pepper
lime wedges and sweet chili sauce,
   to serve

method

1 Place the scallions, ginger, garlic, cilantro, and chile in a
food processor or blender and process until everything
is finely chopped.

2 Transfer the mixture to a mixing bowl, add the chicken,
and combine with the soy sauce, fish sauce, egg white,
flour, lime zest, and black pepper.

3 Heat a little oil in a nonstick skillet and add spoonfuls
of the mixture in batches. Cook each batch for about
4 minutes on each side, until golden and cooked
through. Transfer to a plate and keep warm while
cooking the remaining mixture.

4 Serve the cooked thai chicken cakes with lime wedges
and sweet chili sauce for dipping.

stuffed bell peppers

ingredients

serves 4

4 large red bell peppers
3 tablespoons sunflower oil,
    plus extra for brushing
2 onions, finely chopped
2 garlic cloves, finely chopped
2 fresh green chiles, seeded
    and finely chopped
1–1¼ pound ground round beef
1 teaspoon Tabasco sauce
2 tablespoons all-purpose flour
1 cup beef stock
⅔ cup light cream
1 cup cream cheese
pinch of cayenne pepper
¾ cup golden raisins
salt

method

1 Cut off the tops of the bell peppers, remove the seeds and membranes, then set aside. Cut out the stems from the sliced tops and chop the flesh.

2 Heat the oil in a skillet. Add the onions, garlic, chiles, and chopped bell peppers and cook over low heat, stirring occasionally, for 5 minutes, until softened. Add the beef and Tabasco and season with salt. Increase the heat to medium and cook, stirring frequently and breaking up the meat with a wooden spoon, for 8–10 minutes, until evenly browned. Stir in the flour, then gradually stir in the stock. Bring to a boil, stirring continuously, then reduce the heat, cover, and simmer for 30 minutes.

3 Preheat the oven to 350°F. Brush an ovenproof dish with oil. Spoon the beef mixture into the bell peppers. Stand them upright in the prepared dish and bake in the preheated oven for 45 minutes.

4 Put the cream, cream cheese, and cayenne pepper into a saucepan, season with salt, and stir until smooth. Add the golden raisins and cook over medium heat, stirring continuously, until hot. Do not let the mixture boil.

5 Remove the peppers from the oven and pour the cream cheese sauce over them. Return to the oven and bake for an additional 15 minutes. Serve immediately.

ground beef hash

ingredients

serves 2

4 white round potatoes,
   cut into chunks
12 ounces ground round beef
1 red bell pepper, seeded and
   finely chopped
½ teaspoon sweet paprika
1 tablespoon chopped fresh
   parsley, plus extra to garnish
3 tablespoons sunflower oil
1 onion, finely chopped
2 eggs
salt and pepper

method

1 Cook the potatoes in a saucepan of salted boiling water for 20–25 minutes, until tender but not falling apart. Drain and let cool.

2 Meanwhile, mix together the beef, red bell pepper, paprika, and parsley in a bowl. Season with salt and pepper. Dice the potatoes and add them to the mixture, stirring gently until thoroughly combined.

3 Heat the oil in a large skillet. Add the onion and cook over low heat, stirring occasionally, for 5 minutes, until softened.

4 Add the beef mixture to the skillet and shake the skillet to mix it with the onion, then press down gently with a wooden spoon. Cook over medium heat, without stirring, for 5 minutes, until browned on the underside. Stir well, then cook, without stirring, for 5 minutes. Repeat the stirring and cooking twice until the mixture is evenly browned.

5 Reduce the heat. Make two hollows in the mixture with the back of a spoon. Crack an egg into each hollow, cover, and cook for an additional 5 minutes, until the whites have set. Cut the hash in two, with each half containing an egg, garnish with parsley, and serve immediately.

moroccan-style ground chicken

ingredients

serves 4

2 tablespoons vegetable oil
1 large onion, finely chopped
2 garlic cloves, finely chopped
1 tablespoon ground cumin
1 teaspoon ground cinnamon
2 teaspoons ground turmeric
1 pound fresh ground chicken
2 cups chicken stock
½ cup raisins
1¼ cups couscous
finely grated zest and juice
    of 1 lemon
¼ cup toasted pine nuts
salt and pepper
fresh flat-leaf parsley sprigs,
    to garnish

method

1 Heat the oil in a large, nonstick skillet, add the onion, and cook over low heat, stirring occasionally, for 4–5 minutes, until softened. Add the garlic and spices and cook for an additional minute over medium heat.

2 Add the ground chicken and cook, stirring frequently and breaking up the meat with a wooden spoon, for 4–5 minutes, until lightly browned. Add the stock and raisins, cover, and cook over low heat for an additional 8–10 minutes.

3 Add the couscous, season with salt and pepper, stir, and cover again. Simmer for 5–6 minutes, until the couscous has absorbed the stock and is fully cooked.

4 Remove from the heat, then stir in the lemon zest and juice and pine nuts. Garnish with parsley and serve immediately.

spiced beef & pistachio nuts

ingredients

serves 4

4 tablespoons butter
1 Bermuda onion, chopped
2 garlic cloves, chopped
3 fresh green chiles,
    seeded and chopped
2¼ pounds ground round beef
2 tablespoons coarsely chopped
    pistachio nuts, plus extra
    to garnish
1½ tablespoons garam masala
4 tomatoes, peeled and diced
¼ cup fresh bread crumbs
¼ cup sour cream
salt and pepper

method

1 Preheat the oven to 375°F. Melt the butter in a saucepan. Add the onion, garlic, and chiles and cook over low heat, stirring occasionally, for 5 minutes, until softened. Add the beef, increase the heat to medium, and cook, stirring frequently and breaking it up with a wooden spoon, for 8–10 minutes, until evenly browned.

2 Remove the pan from the heat, stir in the pistachio nuts, garam masala, tomatoes, bread crumbs, and sour cream, and season with salt and pepper. Mix well until thoroughly combined, then spoon the mixture into an ovenproof dish.

3 Bake in the preheated oven for 35–45 minutes, until the top is lightly browned. Serve immediately, garnished with pistachio nuts.

indian-style spicy ground beef

ingredients

serves 4

1 pound ground round beef
1 large onion, finely chopped
2 garlic cloves, crushed
2 white round potatoes, diced
1 teaspoon cumin seeds
2 teaspoons hot chili powder
1 teaspoon ground turmeric
1 teaspoon ground coriander
2 teaspoons garam masala
1 (14½-ounce) can diced tomatoes
1 cup frozen peas
 salt and pepper

to serve

2 tablespoons plain yogurt
4 fresh cilantro sprigs
naan

method

1 Dry-fry the ground beef in a nonstick covered skillet for 4–5 minutes, until browned.

2 Add the onion, garlic, and potatoes and sauté for an additional 1–2 minutes. Add the cumin seeds, chili powder, turmeric, coriander, and garam masala and cook, stirring continuously, for an additional 1–2 minutes.

3 Add the tomatoes and season with salt and pepper, cover, and simmer for 10–12 minutes, until the potatoes are tender.

4 Add the peas and cook for an additional 1–2 minutes. Divide among four dishes, spoon the yogurt over the top, garnish with the cilantro, and serve with naan.

beef curry

ingredients

serves 4

¼ cup peanut oil
1 large onion, finely chopped
1 green bell pepper, seeded
    and diced
1 teaspoon cumin seeds
4 green cardamom pods
2 bay leaves
4 tomatoes, peeled and chopped
2 garlic cloves, finely chopped
1 pound ground round beef
2 teaspoons ground coriander
2 teaspoons ground turmeric
1 teaspoon chili powder
2½ cups beef stock
2 tablespoons chopped
    fresh cilantro
salt
cooked rice and naan, to serve

method

1 Heat half the oil in a large saucepan. Add the onion, green bell pepper, cumin seeds, cardamom pods, and bay leaves and cook over low heat, stirring continuously, for 2–3 minutes, until the spices release their aroma. Add the tomatoes and cook, stirring frequently, for 10 minutes.

2 Meanwhile, heat the remaining oil in a skillet. Add the garlic and cook, stirring frequently, for 1 minute, then add the beef, ground coriander, turmeric, and chili powder. Cook over medium heat, stirring continuously and breaking up the meat with a wooden spoon, for 4–5 minutes, until the meat is evenly browned. Transfer the mixture to the saucepan.

3 Pour in the stock and bring to a boil, then reduce the heat, cover, and simmer, stirring occasionally, for 20–25 minutes. If the mixture seems to be drying out, add a little water.

4 Remove and discard the bay leaves and cardamom pods, then season with salt. Sprinkle with the chopped cilantro and serve immediately with rice and naan.

balti beef curry

ingredients

serves 4

3 tablespoons corn oil
4 onions, thinly sliced
2 garlic cloves, finely chopped
1-inch piece fresh ginger,
    finely chopped
1 teaspoon ground coriander
1 teaspoon chili powder
1 teaspoon ground turmeric
1½ pounds ground round beef
1 cup canned diced tomatoes
2 tablespoons chopped
    fresh cilantro
salt
cooked rice, to serve

method

1 Heat the oil in a skillet. Add the onions, garlic, and ginger and cook over low heat, stirring occasionally, for 5 minutes, until softened. Add the ground coriander, chili powder, and turmeric and cook, stirring occasionally, for an additional 3 minutes.

2 Add the beef, increase the heat to medium, and cook, stirring frequently and breaking it up with a wooden spoon, for 8–10 minutes, until evenly browned. Stir in the tomatoes and season with salt. Reduce the heat, cover, and simmer, stirring occasionally, for 15 minutes. Uncover the pan and cook for an additional 5 minutes.

3 Taste and adjust the seasoning, adding more salt, if needed. Transfer the curry to a warm serving dish, sprinkle with the chopped cilantro, and serve immediately with rice.

spicy beef & sweet potatoes

ingredients

serves 4

4 sweet potatoes
1 (28-ounce) can diced tomatoes
2 fresh green chiles, seeded
    and chopped
6 black peppercorns
6 allspice berries
1 cinnamon stick
1 teaspoon ground coriander
2 tablespoons sunflower oil
1½ pounds ground sirloin beef
1 tablespoon tomato paste
1 onion, finely chopped
1 garlic clove, finely chopped
¼ cup beef stock
salt
sour cream, to serve

method

1 Preheat the oven to 400°F. Prick the sweet potatoes all
over with a fork. Put them directly on an oven shelf and
bake in the preheated oven for 1 hour, until soft. When
they are cool enough to handle, peel off the skins and
chop the flesh.

2 Meanwhile, put the tomatoes, chiles, peppercorns,
allspice berries, cinnamon stick, and ground coriander
into a saucepan and bring to a boil. Reduce the heat
and simmer, stirring occasionally, for 30 minutes.
Discard the cinnamon stick, then press the sauce
through a nylon strainer into a bowl.

3 Heat half the oil in a skillet. Add the beef and cook
over medium heat, stirring frequently and breaking
it up with a wooden spoon, for 8–10 minutes, until
evenly browned. Stir in the tomato mixture and tomato
paste and season with salt. Simmer, stirring frequently,
for 20 minutes.

4 Heat the remaining oil in a skillet. Add the onion and
garlic and cook over low heat, stirring occasionally, for
5 minutes, until softened. Add the sweet potatoes and
stock and cook, stirring continuously, for 5 minutes.
Season with salt and transfer to a warm serving dish.
Top with the beef mixture and serve immediately with
sour cream.

chili con carne

ingredients

serves 6

2 tablespoons corn oil
2 onions, thinly sliced
2 garlic cloves, finely chopped
1½ pounds fresh ground beef
1 (7-ounce) can chopped
    tomatoes
5 tablespoons tomato paste
1 teaspoon ground cumin
1 teaspoon cayenne pepper
1 tablespoon chili powder
1 teaspoon dried oregano
1 bay leaf
1½ cups beef stock
1 (15-ounce) can red kidney
    beans, drained and rinsed
salt
cooked rice, to serve

method

1 Heat the oil in a large saucepan. Add the onions and garlic and cook over low heat, stirring occasionally, for 5 minutes, until softened. Add the beef, increase the heat to medium, and cook, stirring frequently and breaking it up with a wooden spoon, for 8–10 minutes, until evenly browned.

2 Stir in the tomatoes, tomato paste, cumin, cayenne pepper, chili powder, oregano, bay leaf, and stock, then season to taste with salt and bring to a boil. Reduce the heat, cover, and simmer, stirring occasionally, for 1 hour.

3 Add the kidney beans, re-cover the pan and simmer, stirring occasionally, for an additional 30 minutes. Remove and discard the bay leaf and serve immediately with cooked rice.

small bites & nibbles

dim sum

ingredients

makes 20–24

10 ounces ground chicken
½ bunch scallions, trimmed and
    finely chopped
2 tablespoons finely chopped
    fresh cilantro
1 tablespoon soy sauce
1 tablespoon grated fresh ginger
1 tablespoon rice wine vinegar
20–24 wonton wrappers
pepper
sweet chili sauce and dark
    soy sauce, to serve

method

1 Put the ground chicken, scallions, cilantro, soy sauce, ginger, and vinegar into a bowl and use a fork to combine. Season with pepper.

2 Place a teaspoon of the prepared filling in the center of each wonton wrapper. Use your fingers to rub the edges of the wrappers with warm water, gather the two opposite edges to form a tight seal, then bring together the remaining two sides in the middle at the top.

3 Cover the bottom of a bamboo steamer with a single layer of the dim sum. Alternatively, line the bottom of a steamer pan with some parchment paper and cover with the dim sum. Place over a saucepan of boiling water, cover, and steam for 7–8 minutes.

4 Remove from the steam and serve immediately with the chili sauce and soy sauce for dipping.

indonesian beef packages

ingredients

makes 16

4 shallots, finely chopped
2 garlic cloves, finely chopped
1 pound ground round beef
1 teaspoon ground cumin
1 teaspoon ground coriander
2 teaspoons curry powder
2–3 eggs, lightly beaten
all-purpose flour, for dusting
16 sheets phyllo pastry
peanut oil, for brushing
salt and pepper

method

1 Put the shallots, garlic, beef, cumin, ground coriander, and curry powder into a bowl, then season with salt and pepper and mix well until combined. Heat a wok over medium heat, then add the beef mixture and cook, stirring continuously, for 8–10 minutes, until the meat is evenly browned. Remove from the heat and let cool, then stir in just enough of the beaten egg to bind, reserving the remainder.

2 Preheat the oven to 400°F. Lightly dust a baking sheet with flour. Brush one sheet of phyllo with oil, put a second sheet on top, and cut the double layer in half. Put a spoonful of the beef mixture in the center of each piece and fold the sides into the middle. Brush the edges with beaten egg and fold the top and bottom into the middle. Put the packages on the prepared baking sheet and place in the refrigerator while you make more packages in the same way.

3 Brush the tops of the packages with beaten egg and bake in the preheated oven for 20 minutes, until golden brown. Transfer to a warm serving dish and serve immediately.

eggplant rolls

ingredients

serves 4

½ cup olive oil, plus extra
    for brushing
1 onion, grated
1 garlic clove, finely chopped
8 ounces ground round beef
2 tomatoes, peeled, seeded,
    and chopped
3 eggplants, peeled and cut into
    ¼-inch thick slices
6 sheets of phyllo pastry
salt and pepper

cheese sauce

½ cup milk
1 tablespoon butter
2 tablespoons all-purpose flour
1 egg, lightly beaten
¾ cup shredded Swiss cheese,
    Jarlsburg cheese, or
    Muenster cheese
pinch of ground nutmeg

method

1 Heat 2 tablespoons of the oil in a skillet. Add the onion and garlic and cook over low heat, stirring occasionally, for 5 minutes, until softened. Add the beef, increase the heat to medium, and cook, stirring frequently and breaking it up with a wooden spoon, for 8–10 minutes, until evenly browned. Pour off the fat, then add the tomatoes. Season with salt and pepper and simmer gently for 15–20 minutes. Let cool.

2 Meanwhile, make the cheese sauce. Heat the milk, butter, and flour in a saucepan, whisking continuously, until smooth and thick. Stir the egg, cheese, and nutmeg into the sauce, then stir into the beef mixture.

3 Heat half the remaining oil in a skillet. Add the eggplant slices and cook for a few minutes on both sides, until golden brown. Drain on paper towels.

4 Preheat the oven to 350°F. Brush a baking sheet with oil. Stack three sheets of phyllo and brush each with oil. Put half the eggplant slices along one long edge, leaving 2 inches at each end. Top them with half the beef mixture, spreading it evenly, and roll up the phyllo. Repeat to make a second roll. Put the rolls onto the prepared baking sheet and brush with the remaining oil. Bake in the preheated oven for 35–40 minutes, until golden brown. Serve immediately.

mini chimichangas

ingredients

makes about 10

2 tablespoons vegetable oil,
    plus extra for frying
1 onion, finely chopped
8 ounces ground chicken
1 red chile, seeded and
    finely chopped
1 red bell pepper, seeded and
    finely chopped
2/3 cup drained, canned corn kernels
4 scallions, trimmed and
    finely chopped
1/4 cup fresh tomato salsa
10 small flour tortillas
salt and pepper

method

1 Heat 2 tablespoons of the oil in a nonstick skillet, add the onion and ground chicken, and cook for 4–5 minutes, until the chicken starts to brown and the onion is soft.

2 Add the chile and red bell pepper and cook for an additional 2–3 minutes. Remove from the heat and stir in the corn kernels, scallions, and salsa. Season with salt and pepper and place in a bowl. Wipe out the skillet with paper towels.

3 Warm a tortilla briefly on each side in the skillet. Place a large spoonful of the filling in the center, fold in two sides of the tortilla and then the remaining two sides to form a small package. Secure with a toothpick. Repeat with the remaining tortillas and filling.

4 Heat enough oil for frying in a skillet. Add two to three chimichangas and cook for 2 minutes, then turn and cook for an additional 2–3 minutes, until evenly golden brown. Alternatively, heat enough oil for deep-frying in a deep-fat fryer to 350–375°F, or until a cube of bread browns in 30 seconds. Add two to three chimichangas and cook for 2–3 minutes, until golden brown. Drain on paper towels and keep warm while cooking the remaining chimichangas. Serve immediately.

beef samosas

ingredients

makes 28

2 tablespoons sunflower oil,
    plus extra for deep-frying
1 onion, chopped
2 garlic cloves, finely chopped
1½-inch piece fresh ginger, grated
1 teaspoon chili powder
1 teaspoon ground turmeric
1 teaspoon ground coriander
1 teaspoon garam masala
1 pound ground round beef
juice of ½ lemon
3 tablespoons chopped fresh mint
chili sauce, to serve

dough

1¾ cups all-purpose flour,
    plus extra for dusting
large pinch of salt
2 tablespoons sunflower oil
about ⅓ cup warm water

method

1 For the dough, sift together the flour and salt into a bowl. Make a well in the center and pour in the oil and water. Gradually incorporate the dry ingredients into the liquid, adding more water, if necessary. Invert onto a lightly floured surface and knead until smooth and elastic. Shape into a ball and let rest for 30 minutes.

2 Meanwhile, heat the oil in a large skillet. Add the onion, garlic, and ginger and cook over low heat, stirring occasionally, for 5 minutes, until softened. Stir in the chili powder, turmeric, ground coriander, and garam masala and cook, stirring occasionally, for 3 minutes. Add the beef, increase the heat to medium, and cook, stirring frequently and breaking it up with a wooden spoon, for 8–10 minutes, until evenly browned. Stir in the lemon juice and mint and let cool.

3 Divide the dough into 14 pieces. Roll out each piece into an oval about 8 inches long. Cut in half widthwise, brush the straight edge with water, and fold in each side to make a cone. Put a tablespoonful of the beef mixture into each cone, brush the open side with water, and press to seal. Heat enough oil for deep-frying in a deep-fat fryer to 350–375°F, or until a cube of bread browns in 30 seconds. Cook the samosas, in batches, until crisp and golden brown. Serve with chili sauce.

beef & pine nut triangles

ingredients

makes 15

1 tablespoon olive oil
1 small onion, chopped
2 garlic cloves, finely chopped
1 teaspoon ground coriander
1 teaspoon ground cumin
10 ounces ground round beef
1/4 cup chopped fresh mint
2 tablespoons pine nuts
2 potatoes, cut into chunks
1/2 cup shredded American cheese
    or cheddar cheese
1 stick butter, melted
10 sheets phyllo pastry
salt
tomato and basil salsa, to serve

method

1 Heat the oil in a large skillet. Add the onion and garlic and cook over low heat, stirring occasionally, for 5 minutes, until softened. Stir in the coriander and cumin and cook, stirring occasionally, for an additional 3 minutes. Add the beef, half the mint, and the pine nuts. Increase the heat to medium and cook, stirring and breaking up the meat with a wooden spoon, for 8–10 minutes, until evenly browned. Season with salt.

2 Meanwhile, cook the potatoes in a saucepan of salted boiling water for 15–20 minutes, until tender but not falling apart. Drain, transfer to a bowl, and mash well, then stir in the cheese until melted. Stir in the beef mixture.

3 Preheat the oven to 400°F. Brush two baking sheets with melted butter. Brush one sheet of phyllo with melted butter, put a second sheet on top, and brush with more melted butter. Cut the double layer lengthwise into three strips. Put a heaping tablespoon of the filling near one end of a strip, then fold over the corner to form a triangle. Continue to fold over in triangles to make a neat package, then place on a prepared baking sheet. Make another 14 triangles in the same way. Brush with melted butter and bake in the preheated oven for 8–10 minutes, until golden brown. Serve with a warm tomato and basil salsa.

beef-filled pancakes

ingredients

serves 4

2 tablespoons sunflower oil,
    plus extra for brushing
1 onion, chopped
2 carrots, grated
1 pound ground round beef
1 tablespoon tomato paste
1 tablespoon all-purpose flour
1¼ cups hot beef stock
salt and pepper

thin pancake batter
1 cup all-purpose flour
pinch of salt
1 egg, lightly beaten
1¼ cups milk
1 teaspoon sunflower oil

method

1 First, make the pancake batter. Sift the flour and salt into a bowl, then add the egg and half the milk and beat until smooth. Stir in the remaining milk and the oil (this will make a thin batter). Set aside.

2 Heat the oil in a skillet. Add the onion and carrots and cook over low heat, stirring occasionally, for 5 minutes, until softened. Add the beef, increase the heat to medium, and cook, stirring frequently and breaking it up with a wooden spoon, for 8–10 minutes, until evenly browned. Stir the tomato paste and flour into the stock and add to the skillet. Season with salt and pepper, reduce the heat, and simmer, stirring occasionally, for 30 minutes.

3 Meanwhile, brush a skillet with oil and heat. Stir the batter and pour a little into the center of the skillet, then tilt and rotate the pan to cover the bottom evenly. Cook for 1–1½ minutes, until the bottom is golden brown, then flip over the pancake and cook the other side for 30 seconds. Make more pancakes with the remaining batter, brushing the skillet with oil as required.

4 Preheat the oven to 375°F. Divide the beef filling among the pancakes and roll them up. Put them into a greased ovenproof dish in a single layer and bake in the preheated oven for 15 minutes. Serve immediately.

beef in pita pockets

ingredients

serves 4

2 tablespoons olive oil
1 onion, chopped
1 garlic clove, chopped
1 pound ground round beef
1 cup canned diced tomatoes
1 teaspoon ground cumin
1 teaspoon ground coriander
$\frac{1}{2}$ teaspoon ground turmeric
$\frac{2}{3}$ cup pine nuts
2 tablespoons chopped
    fresh cilantro
salt and pepper

to serve

8 pita breads, warmed
chopped cucumber
shredded lettuce
sour cream

method

1 Heat the oil in a skillet. Add the onion and garlic and cook over low heat, stirring occasionally, for 5 minutes, until softened. Add the beef, increase the heat to medium, and cook, stirring frequently and breaking it up with a wooden spoon, for 8–10 minutes, until evenly browned. Stir in the tomatoes, cumin, ground coriander, and turmeric. Season with salt and pepper, reduce the heat, and simmer, stirring occasionally, for 15–20 minutes.

2 Meanwhile, dry-fry the pine nuts in a small skillet, stirring continuously, until golden. Stir the pine nuts and chopped cilantro into the meat mixture and simmer for 3–4 minutes.

3 To serve, cut a slit in the side of each pita bread to make a pocket. Put a little of the beef mixture into each pocket with some chopped cucumber and shredded lettuce. Top with a spoonful of sour cream and serve immediately.

thai chicken pastries

ingredients

makes 20

2 tablespoons peanut oil
1 onion, finely chopped
1 garlic clove, finely chopped
½-inch piece fresh ginger,
    finely chopped
2 fresh red chiles, seeded and
    finely chopped
1 teaspoon chili powder
½ teaspoon ground coriander
½ teaspoon ground turmeric
8 ounces ground chicken
1 tomato, peeled and diced
⅓ cup frozen peas, thawed
2 tablespoons lime juice
2 sheets ready-to-bake puff pastry,
    thawed if frozen
all-purpose flour, for dusting
1 egg, lightly beaten
salt

method

1 Heat the oil in a skillet. Add the onion, garlic, ginger, and chiles and cook over low heat, stirring occasionally, for 5 minutes, until softened. Stir in the chili powder, ground coriander, and turmeric, season with salt, and cook, stirring occasionally, for an additional 3 minutes.

2 Add the chicken, increase the heat to medium, and cook, stirring frequently and breaking it up with a wooden spoon, for 8–10 minutes, until evenly browned. Stir in the tomato, peas, and lime juice, reduce the heat, and cook, stirring occasionally, for an additional 5 minutes. Remove the skillet from the heat

3 Preheat the oven to 400°F. Roll out the pastry on a lightly floured surface to a thickness of about ⅛ inch. Stamp out 20 circles with a 4-inch pastry cutter. Put 2 teaspoons of the chicken mixture on one side of each circle. Brush the edges with water and fold over, pressing together the edges to seal. Crimp the edges with a fork. Put the pastries on a baking sheet, brush with the beaten egg, and bake in the preheated oven for 20–30 minutes, until golden brown.

4 Remove from the oven, transfer to a wire rack, and let cool slightly. Serve warm.

beef & onion piroshki

ingredients

makes 40–45

4 tablespoons butter, plus extra
    for greasing
1 onion, finely chopped
8 ounces ground round beef
⅓ cup cooked rice
2 tablespoons sour cream
1 teaspoon Worcestershire sauce
1 teaspoon caraway seeds
1 hard-boiled egg, chopped
1 egg, beaten with
    1 teaspoon water
salt and pepper

dough

2¾ cups all-purpose flour,
    plus extra for dusting
pinch of salt
¼ cup cream cheese
1 stick butter
about 3 tablespoons water
3 tablespoons heavy cream

method

1 For the dough, sift the flour and salt into a bowl. Add the cream cheese and butter and rub in with your fingertips until the mixture resembles bread crumbs. Add the water and cream 1 tablespoon at a time. Knead gently, adding more water, if necessary. Shape into a ball, cover, and chill in the refrigerator for 30 minutes.

2 Meanwhile, melt the butter in a saucepan. Add the onion and cook over low heat, stirring occasionally, for 5 minutes, until softened. Add the beef, increase the heat to medium, and cook, stirring frequently and breaking it up with a wooden spoon, for 8–10 minutes, until evenly browned. Remove the pan from the heat, stir in the rice, sour cream, Worcestershire sauce, caraway seeds, and chopped egg, and season with salt and pepper.

3 Preheat the oven to 400°F. Grease two baking sheets with butter. Roll out the dough to a thickness of about ⅛ inch on a lightly floured surface. Stamp out circles with a 3¼-inch plain cutter. Put a teaspoon of the filling on one side of each circle. Brush the edges of the circles with the beaten egg, then fold over the dough. Press together the edges to seal and crimp with a fork. Place on the prepared baking sheets and brush with the beaten egg. Bake in the preheated oven for 20 minutes, until golden brown. Serve immediately.

beef croquettes

ingredients

serves 6

9 russet potatoes (2¼ pounds),
    cut into chunks
1 onion, finely chopped
1 pound ground round beef
1 tablespoon snipped fresh chives
1 tablespoon chopped
    fresh parsley
2 teaspoons Worcestershire sauce
    or ketchup
3 eggs
3 tablespoons all-purpose flour
4 cups fresh bread crumbs
sunflower oil, for shallow-frying
salt and pepper

method

1 Cook the potatoes in a large saucepan of salted boiling water for 20–25 minutes, until tender but not falling apart. Drain well, transfer to a bowl, and mash the potatoes until smooth.

2 Add the onion, beef, chives, parsley, and Worcestershire sauce and season with salt and pepper. Mix well until thoroughly combined. Cover the bowl with plastic wrap and chill the mixture in the refrigerator for 30–45 minutes, until firm.

3 Dampen your hands and shape the mixture into 12 log-shape croquettes. Lightly beat the eggs in a shallow dish, spread out the flour in a second shallow dish, and spread out the bread crumbs in a third shallow dish.

4 Pour oil into a large skillet to a depth of about ½ inch and heat. Meanwhile, coat the croquettes first in the flour, then in the beaten egg, and, finally, in the bread crumbs. Shake off any excess.

5 Add the croquettes to the skillet, in batches, if necessary, and cook over medium heat, turning occasionally, for 8–10 minutes, until crisp, evenly browned, and cooked through. Remove from the skillet with a spatula and keep warm while you cook the remaining croquettes. Serve immediately.

spanish meatballs

ingredients

serves 4–6

1 pound ground chuck beef
½ cup long-grain rice, cooked,
    cooled, and chilled
1 onion, finely chopped
1 garlic clove, crushed
1 egg, beaten
3 tablespoons finely chopped
    fresh flat-leaf parsley
vegetable oil, for frying
salt and pepper
pita breads and salad greens,
    to serve

method

1 Put the ground beef, rice, onion, garlic, egg, and parsley into a bowl and use your fingertips to combine. Season with salt and pepper. Shape the mixture into 18–20 small meatballs, place on a baking sheet, cover, and chill for 20–30 minutes.

2 Heat the oil in a skillet, add the meatballs in two batches and cook, turning regularly, for about 12–14 minutes, until thoroughly cooked.

3 Serve in pita breads with salad greens.

beef & mozzarella risotto balls

ingredients

serves 4

1½ cups long-grain rice
4 tablespoons butter
2 tablespoons grated Parmesan
    cheese
1 tablespoon chopped fresh
    parsley
1 tablespoon olive oil
1 shallot, finely chopped
1 garlic clove, finely chopped
4 ounces ground round beef
½ cup dry white wine
2 tablespoons tomato paste
4 ounces mozzarella cheese,
    cut into cubes
2 eggs
½ cup all-purpose flour
sunflower oil, for deep-frying
salt and pepper

method

1 Cook the rice in a large saucepan of salted boiling water according to the package directions, until tender. Drain, rinse with boiling water, and return to the pan. Stir in half the butter, the Parmesan, and parsley. Spread out on a baking sheet and let cool.

2 Meanwhile, melt the remaining butter with the olive oil in a saucepan. Add the shallot and garlic and cook over low heat, stirring occasionally, for 5 minutes, until softened. Add the beef, increase the heat to medium, and cook, stirring frequently and breaking it up with a wooden spoon, for 5–8 minutes, until evenly browned. Stir in the wine and cook for 5 minutes. Reduce the heat and stir in the tomato paste, then cover and simmer for 15 minutes. Season with salt and pepper.

3 When the rice is cold, shape into balls. Make a small hollow in each and put a spoonful of meat mixture and a cube of cheese inside, then reshape to enclose the filling. Lightly beat the eggs in a dish and spread out the flour in a separate dish. Dip the balls in the egg and then in the flour. Heat enough sunflower oil for deep-frying in a deep-fat fryer to 350–375°F, or until a cube of bread browns in 30 seconds. Deep-fry the balls, in batches, until golden brown, and serve immediately.

beef & herb patties

ingredients

serves 6

2 tablespoons sunflower oil
1 Bermuda onion, finely chopped
2 garlic cloves, finely chopped
2¼ pounds ground round beef
3 eggs
2 tablespoons sour cream
1 tablespoon chopped fresh
    flat-leaf parsley, plus extra
    sprigs to garnish
1 teaspoon sweet paprika
2 cups fresh bread crumbs
6 tablespoons butter
salt and pepper

method

1 Heat the oil in a skillet. Add the onion and garlic and cook over low heat, stirring occasionally, for 8–10 minutes, until golden brown.

2 Transfer the onion and garlic to a large bowl, add the beef, one of the eggs, the sour cream, chopped parsley, paprika, and ½ cup of the bread crumbs, and season with salt and pepper. Using your hands, mix well until all the ingredients are thoroughly combined. Form the mixture into 12 disk-shape patties.

3 Lightly beat the remaining eggs in a shallow dish and spread out the remaining bread crumbs in a separate shallow dish. Coat the patties first in beaten egg and then in bread crumbs.

4 Melt the butter in a large skillet. Add the patties, in batches, if necessary, and cook over medium heat for 5–6 minutes on each side, until evenly browned and thoroughly cooked. Remove from the skillet with a spatula and keep warm while you cook the remaining patties. Garnish with parsley sprigs and serve immediately.

indian potato cakes

ingredients

makes 10

9 russet potatoes (2¼ pounds),
    cut into chunks
½ cup peanut oil
1 large onion, finely chopped
2 garlic cloves, finely chopped
2 fresh green chiles, seeded
    and finely chopped
1½-inch piece fresh ginger,
    finely chopped
1 teaspoon ground cumin
1 teaspoon ground coriander
2 tablespoons chopped fresh mint
1 tablespoon chopped fresh
    cilantro
8 ounces ground round beef
⅓ cup frozen peas, thawed
¼ cup lemon juice
2 eggs
2 cups fresh bread crumbs
salt

method

1 Cook the potatoes in a large saucepan of salted boiling
water for 20–25 minutes, until tender but not falling
apart. Drain, return to the pan, and mash well.

2 Heat 1 tablespoon of the oil in a large skillet. Add the
onion, garlic, chiles, ginger, cumin, ground coriander,
mint, and chopped cilantro and cook over low heat,
stirring occasionally, for 5 minutes. Add the beef,
increase the heat to medium, and cook, stirring
frequently and breaking it up with a wooden spoon, for
5 minutes. Add the peas and cook, stirring frequently,
for an additional 3–5 minutes, until the meat is evenly
browned and the mixture is dry. Remove from the heat,
season with salt, and stir in the lemon juice.

3 Divide the mashed potato into ten portions. Put one
portion in your hand and flatten it into a circle. Put a
spoonful of the beef mixture in the middle and reshape
to enclose the filling. Make another nine in the same way.

4 Lightly beat the eggs in a shallow dish. Spread out
the bread crumbs in a separate shallow dish. Dip the
potato cakes in the beaten egg and then in the bread
crumbs to coat. Chill in the refrigerator for 30 minutes.

5 Heat the remaining oil in a skillet. Add the potato cakes,
in batches, and cook over medium heat, turning
occasionally, until golden brown. Serve immediately.

fried beef dumplings with tomato sauce

ingredients

serves 6

1½ pounds ground chuck beef
1 cup shredded beef suet or
  shortening
¼ cup finely chopped onion
½ teaspoon ground ginger
¼ teaspoon ground cloves
¼ teaspoon ground nutmeg
1 extra-large egg, lightly beaten
1 cup rolled oats
vegetable oil, for deep-frying
salt and pepper

tomato sauce

2 tablespoons sunflower oil
1 onion, finely chopped
2 garlic cloves, finely chopped
2 tablespoons tomato paste
½ cup water
1 (14½-ounce) can diced tomatoes

method

1 First, make the tomato sauce. Heat the oil in a saucepan, add the onion and garlic, and cook over low heat, stirring occasionally, for 5 minutes, until softened. Add the tomato paste, water, and tomatoes and bring to a boil, then reduce the heat, and simmer for 15–20 minutes.

2 Put the beef, suet, and onion into a bowl and mix well. Add the spices, season with salt and pepper, and mix well again. Finally, add the egg and mix until thoroughly combined.

3 Break off pieces of the mixture and shape into 2-inch balls. Spread out the oats in a shallow dish and roll the dumplings in it until coated.

4 Heat enough oil for deep-frying in a deep-fat fryer to 350–375°F, or until a cube of bread browns in 30 seconds. Add the dumplings and cook for 8–10 minutes, until brown and thoroughly cooked.

5 Remove the dumplings and drain well. Transfer to a warm serving dish and serve immediately with the tomato sauce.

crispy beef fritters

ingredients

serves 4

4 eggs, separated
8 ounces ground round beef
1 small onion, finely chopped
½ teaspoon baking powder
2 tablespoons chopped fresh
    parsley
1 tablespoon Worcestershire sauce
¼ cup sunflower oil
salt and pepper

method

1 Beat the egg yolks in a large bowl until pale and thick. Fold in the beef, onion, baking powder, parsley, and Worcestershire sauce and season with salt and pepper. Stir gently until thoroughly combined.

2 Whisk the egg whites in a separate grease-free bowl until stiff, then gently fold them into the beef mixture.

3 Heat the oil in a large skillet. Drop tablespoonfuls of the beef mixture, about four at a time, into the hot oil and cook for 3 minutes, or until puffed up and brown at the edges. Using a spatula or slotted spoon, turn the fritters over and cook for an additional 2–3 minutes.

4 Remove with a slotted spoon and drain on paper towels. Keep warm while you cook the remaining fritters, then serve immediately.

stuffed beef rolls

ingredients

serves 4

6 ounces ground round beef
1 shallot, finely chopped
2 tablespoons butter
½ cup fresh bread crumbs
grated rind of 1 lemon
6 green olives, pitted and chopped
1 egg, lightly beaten
8 slices bottom round roast beef,
    each about ¼ inch thick
2 tablespoons olive oil
2 onions, finely chopped
1 garlic clove, finely chopped
2 carrots, finely chopped
1¼ cups beef stock
2 tomatoes, peeled, seeded,
    and sliced
1 bay leaf
3 tablespoons finely chopped
    fresh parsley
salt and pepper

method

1 Preheat the oven to 350°F. Put the ground beef, shallot, butter, bread crumbs, lemon rind, and olives into a bowl and mix well. Add the egg, then season with salt and pepper and mix until thoroughly combined. Divide the mixture among the beef slices, then roll up and tie with kitchen string.

2 Heat the oil in a flameproof casserole dish. Add the beef rolls, in batches, and cook over low–medium heat, turning occasionally, until browned all over. Remove with a slotted spoon and set aside.

3 Add the onions, garlic, and carrots to the casserole dish and cook over low heat, stirring occasionally, for 5 minutes. Add the stock, tomatoes, and bay leaf and bring to a boil. Remove the casserole dish from the heat and return the beef rolls to it, then cover and cook in the preheated oven for 1½ hours.

4 Remove the casserole dish from the oven and lift out the beef rolls. Carefully remove and discard the string and put the rolls on a warm serving plate. Strain the cooking liquid into a small bowl, pressing down on the vegetables with the back of a spoon. Taste and adjust the seasoning, adding salt and pepper, if needed, then pour the sauce over the beef rolls. Sprinkle with the parsley and serve immediately.

meatballs on sticks

ingredients

serves 6–8

4 pork and herb Italian-style
   sausages
4 ounces ground chuck beef
2 cups fresh white bread crumbs
1 onion, finely chopped
1 teaspoon finely chopped parsley
1 teaspoon finely chopped thyme
1 teaspoon finely chopped sage
1 egg
sunflower oil, for brushing
salt and pepper

method

1 Preheat the broiler to medium–high, or alternatively preheat the barbecue. Remove the sausage meat from the casings, place in a large bowl, and break up with a fork. Add the ground beef, bread crumbs, onion, herbs, and egg. Season with salt and pepper and stir well with a wooden spoon until thoroughly mixed.

2 Form the mixture into small balls, about the size of a golf ball, between the palms of your hands. Spear each meatball with a toothpick and brush with oil.

3 Cook under the preheated broiler, or over medium–hot coals, turning frequently and brushing with more oil as necessary, for 10 minutes, or until thoroughly cooked. Serve immediately.